Events That Changed the Course of History

THE STORY OF

FLORIDA

Becoming a State

75 Years Later

By Hannah Litwiller

EVENTS THAT CHANGED THE COURSE OF HISTORY: THE STORY OF FLORIDA BECOMING A STATE 75 YEARS LATER

1405 SW 6th Avenue • Ocala, Florida 34471 • Phone 352-622-1825 Fax 352-622-1875
Website: www.atlantic-pub.com • Email: sales@atlantic-pub.com
SAN Number: 268-1250

Library of Congress Cataloging-in-Publication Data
Names: Litwiller, Hannah, 1994- author.
Title: The story of Florida becoming a state 175 years later / by: Hannah Litwiller.
Other titles: Events that changed the course of history.
Description: Ocala, Florida : Atlantic Publishing Group, Inc., [2018] |
  Series: Events that changed the course of history | Audience: 9-12. |
  Includes bibliographical references.
Identifiers: LCCN 2018023601| ISBN 9781620235454 (pbk.) | ISBN 9781620235478
  (library edition) | ISBN 9781620235461 (ebook)
Subjects: LCSH: Florida--History--Juvenile literature.
Classification: LCC F311.3 .L58 2018 | DDC 975.9--dc23
LC record available at https://lccn.loc.gov/2018023601

Printed in the United States

PROJECT MANAGER: Danielle Lieneman
INTERIOR LAYOUT: Nicole Sturk

Over the years, we have adopted a number of dogs from rescues and shelters. First there was Bear and after he passed, Ginger and Scout. Now, we have Kira, another rescue. They have brought immense joy and love not just into our lives, but into the lives of all who met them.

We want you to know a portion of the profits of this book will be donated in Bear, Ginger and Scout's memory to local animal shelters, parks, conservation organizations, and other individuals and nonprofit organizations in need of assistance.

– *Douglas & Sherri Brown,*
President & Vice-President of Atlantic Publishing

Table of Contents

Introduction

"It's always sunny in the Sunshine State. Except for at night."
— Jarod Kintz

When you read the word "Florida", what do you picture?

Can you feel the sand between your toes on one of Florida's famous beaches like Fort Lauderdale or Cocoa Beach? Do you think about riding roller coasters at Universal Studios or meeting Mickey Mouse at Disney World? What about enjoying a worry-free life in the Florida Keys or exploring the wetlands at Everglades National Park?

I'll be honest: that's what I think about when I imagine Florida. I can feel the cool breeze of the ocean and smell the palm trees in the air. Thinking about Florida reminds me of vacation and relaxation, somewhere where I can wear a swimsuit year-round. So, imagine my surprise when I learned that there's more to Florida than beaches and theme parks!

Believe it or not, Florida has a fascinating history. Although it is not considered one of the original 13 colonies of the United States, the state was "discovered" by Western civilization in the 16th century and had its own part to play during the American Revolution. Numerous Native American tribes and cultures once flourished there. Spain, France, England, and the emerging United States all claimed territory on the peninsula, and bitter wars were fought between nations to take over the area.

Yes, it's true: there's a lot more history to Florida than just the construction of Disney World.

A map of the state of Florida.

Florida became a state only 175 years ago, but the road from wild, unconquered lands to a U.S. state began much earlier. From the Spanish conquistadors' explorations to the Civil War's battlegrounds, Florida's history contains much more than a simple signed document and a proclamation of statehood. The Native American tribes that made the swamps and grasslands their home are just as important as the United States figureheads that took over the territory and claimed it as their own. Those who built and lived in Fort Mose, the first settlement for free slaves, deserve recognition for their determination and willpower to overcome the swamps of an unfamiliar land. There are so many stories to be told about the people who conquered, settled, or relocated to Florida, and they all have a part to play in the history of Florida's statehood.

Writing a book — and learning about Florida in the process — has been a huge adventure. I hope you, too, learn about the history of the Sunshine State, and I implore you to continue learning about the people who made Florida what it is. I think it is a fascinating story, and I hope you agree.

Thank you for joining me on this adventure.

Viva la Florida!

Chapter 1
Indigenous Peoples in Florida

"Sometimes I think I've figured out some order in the universe, but then I find myself in Florida."
— Susan Orlean

Florida has been home to bugs, reptiles, birds, and mammals for millennia, but the people who first moved to the peninsula may have happened upon the area by chance.

The first early peoples of Florida entered North America from eastern Asia about 12,000 years ago. A low sea level meant that a large land bridge was exposed between Siberia and Alaska, now known as the Bering Strait. Ancient hunter-gathers, looking for food and animals to kill, crossed that land bridge that connected Asia to North America. This bridge was about the distance from Orlando to New York City.

Those first people are known as Paleoindians, and they made their way to Florida around 10,000 B.C. They were nomadic, moving quickly across the land area that is now the United States and Canada. Campsites of the Paleoindians can still be found from Alaska to Southern Florida.

During that time, Florida had more land mass due to the lowered sea level — the Florida shoreline on the Gulf of Mexico was nearly 100 miles larger. Florida was also much drier and less swamp-like. Plants that grew in Florida back then could survive in Nebraska's arid prairies today, meaning that the wildlife of ancient Florida was different than the enormous alligators that currently inhabit the Everglades and make up the TV show River Monsters.

 Paleo sound familiar? It should — the Paleo Diet requires that all consumption of food must be food that was available or consumed by humans during the Paleolithic era.

The first Floridians hunted animals like bison, camels, mastodons, and mammoths, but when their hunting wiped out those populations of large mammals, they settled for the always-plentiful rabbits and deer. Fresh water, a precious commodity, was scarce back then, so the Paleoindians settled around watering holes or shallow lakes from which they knew their prey would drink, such as the Warm Mineral Springs in present-day Sarasota.[1] They hunted, butchered, and consumed animals in these areas, and the artifacts that remain from these activities, like a giant tortoise cooked in its shell at Little Salt Spring around 12,000 years ago, are studied by modern archaeologists.

The Paleoindians continued this way of life until around 9,000 B.C. when the glaciers melted. Florida's climate provided more water sources, but the rising ocean meant that coastal areas were flooded and the landmass began to shrink. With less land and a growing human population, the Paleoindians began to follow a less nomadic way of life. They camped in one area

1. Clark, 2014

much longer and moved between water sources less frequently. These larger campsites have been found near Tampa, around Paynes Prairie south of Gainsville, Silver Springs, and at other locations around Northern Florida.

Over time, the "tool kits" of the Paleoindians changed as they began to acclimate to the new environmental conditions. The tools became more advanced and stone tools were used more often. As their weapons changed, their culture did too. This led to a new era in 7,500 B.C. named the Archaic period.

Archaic Peoples

Although the environment of the Archaic period was wetter than that experienced in the Paleo era, the climate was still drier than that of present-day Florida. Archaic campsites are also studied by archeologists, including an amazing find by Glen Doran and David Fickel from Florida State University. Astoundingly, they uncovered a human burial ground in the bottom of a shallow pond in the Windover Pond site in Brevard County. After performing radiocarbon dating on the bones, it was estimated that the humans had lived around 7,000 years ago.

The pond contained peat, which is an accumulation of partially decayed vegetation or organic matter and was able to preserve the bodies found in the swamp. The remains found included the bones of 168 people: men and women of all ages from babies to those around 60 years old.

The peat preserved the bodies so well that scientists were able to tell what the humans' cause of death was and their former living conditions. They could even tell that one 15-year-old boy had been paralyzed from the waist down before his death. By 1984, scientists realized that they could extract the DNA from the brains of a few of the bodies, learning that many of those buried belonged to the same family. They had been burying their dead in the pond for over a century!

Other artifacts that were found included shark and dog teeth attached to wooden handles and tools from deer bone or bobcat bone. Plants were preserved, such as a wild gourds refashioned into a dipper for water. Fiber fabrics and matting that were probably used for weaving clothes were also found. These findings tell archaeologists that the Archaic people had begun to assemble items that helped them adapt to their surroundings in Florida.

By 5,000 B.C., the climate had changed again and become more like modern conditions as we know them today. The populations of Archaics increased, and they practiced a more settled way of life. By 3,000 B.C., their population occupied almost every part of the state — later Archaic sites have been found in northwest, southwest, and northeast Florida, as well as in the St. Johns River Drainage. These sites can often be recognized by the large amounts of collected mollusk shells, a common, tasty meal for the Archaics.

By 2,000 B.C., the Archaics learned to make fired-clay pottery, or pottery that is shaped and then heated to remove moisture. They also used Spanish moss of palmetto fibers to supplement their pottery. Those artifacts, some adorned with massive shells, have been found throughout the entire state.

As their populations spread across the Florida region, the Archaic culture began to grow and change with different groups. Their excavated pottery often reveals specificities of each of their cultures and are used to define and name the tribes that began to form their own identities around 500 B.C. Different groups made their ceramic vessels in specific shapes and decorated them in unique designs. Each regional culture with its distinct style of pottery often lived in their own distinct area of Florida. Each had its own unique practices and customs that reflected the region.[2] Although this chapter only discusses two specifically, there were at least 40 different groups living in Florida before the Spanish "discovered" it.

Timucua Tribe

One of the largest tribes were the Timucuans, who were based in northern Florida. The tribe was enormous — at one time, there were 35 chiefdoms. The various groups of Timucua spoke multiple dialects of the same language and are categorized into the eastern and western groups. The Eastern Timucua were located along the Atlantic coast; the Western Timucua lived around the Florida peninsula, all the way to the Aucilla River.

Timucua Indians at a feast.

2. Gannon, 1996

Timacua Traditions

The different Timucua tribes often had their own individual cultures, but some traditions were homogeneous throughout the tribes. The Timucua tribes in Northeast Florida lived in villages of 30 houses and 200 to 300 people. The circular 15-foot houses were made of upright poles lining the sides, and palm leaves were used to thatch the roof. Smoke was released through a hole in the roof.

A council house, which could hold up to 3,000 villagers, was common in larger Timacua villages. If a village became too large, some families would leave to start a new village nearby, remaining loyal to the original. Wartime alliances between these brother villages were typical.[3]

The Timucua were a semi-agricultural group and primarily planted maize and tobacco. Beans, squash, and other vegetables were planted and used as part of their diet. Corn was ground into flour and used to make fritters. The tribe planted crops after clearing weeds and brush with fire. Then women would plant seeds with a tool made of two sticks, called a coa.

In addition to agriculture, the men would hunt and collect meat from alligators, manatees, fish, and freshwater and saltwater shellfish. The women gathered fruits and nuts and baked bread from the koonti root. Meat was cooked over an open fire, called the barbacoa, or boiled; fish were dried or boiled.

Barbacoa is the origin of the word barbeque!

3. Manataka, n.d

A black tea (known as a White Drink because of its purifying effects) was served at ceremonies. It was tea brewed from the leaves of the Yaupon plant with a very high concentration of caffeine and was only consumed by high-up males tribe. Those who drank it often vomited immediately, so, as a result, the tribe believed the drink was purifying. The tea was essential to most Timucua rituals and hunts.

The Timucua's time wasn't only spent hunting for food or juice-cleansing — they also played games like the "Apalachee ball game". Two teams made up of 40 to 50 players would kick a ball at a goal post. If they hit the post, they scored one point, but if they landed it in the eagle's nest perched at the top of the post, they'd win two points. The first team to score 11 points won. The eastern Timucua played similarly but would throw the ball instead of kicking it. Other pastimes included archery, running, and dancing.

When the Spanish conquistadors arrived, they were shocked by the Timucua's appearance. They were giants compared to the Spanish — often around 4 inches taller than the Europeans. The men of the tribe also wore their hair in a bun, which only added to their height. Each member was covered in tattoos, which were earned according to their deeds — kind of like a permanent Boy Scout patch. Even children were tattooed as they took on more responsibility. The tattoos were given by poking individual holes in the skin and rubbing ashes into the wounds.

Calusa Tribe

The Calusa were another Native American people that lived along Florida's southwest coast. Like other indigenous cultures that inhabited Florida for millennia, the Calusas developed from the Archaic peoples of the Everglades region.

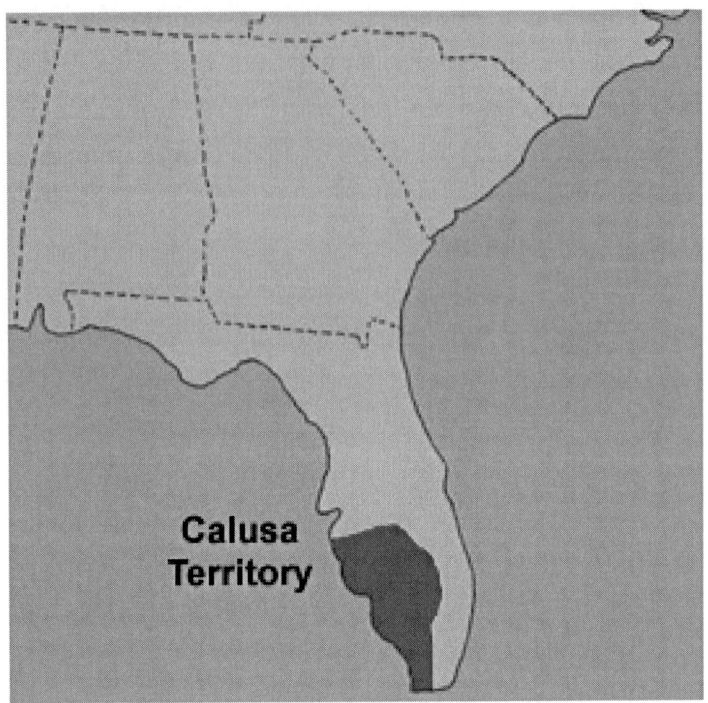

The territory in Florida of the Calusa Indians.

Calusa territory ranged from Cape Sable to Charlotte Harbor, Charlotte and Lee counties, and perhaps even the Florida Keys. They were the largest tribe by population in southern Florida, and they held political influence and control over other tribes in the region like the Mayaimi, the Tequesta, and the Jaega.

According to Hernando de Escalante Fontaneda, a Spanish man held captive by the tribe, Calusa meant "fierce people." Smaller tribes were constantly on the lookout for the Calusa; once the Spanish arrived, they, too, soon became targets of Calusa attacks.

Calusa Culture

Rather than raising crops to survive, the Calusa developed a complex system based on estuarine fisheries. An estuary is a partially enclosed body of water with one or more rivers or streams flowing into it and a free connection to the open sea. The Calusa used these to their advantage, easily catching seafood and shellfish.

To protect themselves from rain and flooding, they built their homes on stilts and wove Palmetto leaves to waterproof their roofs, though their huts had no walls. The men fished with nets, speared eels and turtles, and used fish-bone arrowheads to hunt deer. The women and children caught shellfish like crabs, conches, and oysters.

Unlike other tribes, the Calusa did not make much pottery — instead, they collected shells from their bounties. The shells were used as ornaments for their religious shrines and for tools, utensils, and jewelry. Mounds of shells can still be found today in southern Florida, like shell and clay mound in Mound Key at Estero Bay. It is thought that Calos, where the leader of the tribe lived, was located there.

The Calusa society was complex and consisted of both commoners and nobles. A few leaders, such as the tribal chief, a military leader, and a chief priest, governed the tribe.

The Calusa lived in two-story, communal houses. Spanish visitors said that the chief's house could hold 2,000 villagers easily, often serving as the council house. When the chief welcomed the Spanish into his home, he and his sister-wife sat on raised seats surrounded by 500 men and 500 women, respectively. In 1697, the Spanish mentioned that Calos, the Calusa captial, had 16 residences, each of which housed 1,000 residents.

Living on the coast made the Calusa excellent sailors. Their main waterway was the Calooshahatchee River, which means "River of the Calusa." Using dugout canoes made from 15-foot hollowed-out cypress logs, they traveled as far as Cuba, attacking ships close to shore and looking for wrecked ships along the coastline in search for treasure.[4]

The Calusa wore little clothing due to the oppressively humid Florida heat. The men wore a deerskin loincloth and kept their hair long. The women wore Spanish moss skirts. The Calusa painted their bodies, and it was once recorded that the chief's wife was adorned with precious stones, pearls, and gold beads around her neck. The chief's son wore beads on his legs and a gold ornament on his forehead.[5]

The Calusa's religion and belief system were integral to their culture and way of life. They believed that three otherworldly beings ruled the Earth. The most powerful ruler of the supernatural beings was in charge of the planet, the second oversaw human politics, and the last was a warlord who would choose which tribe won in battle.

The Calusa also believed that humans had three souls: the pupil, the shadow, and the reflection. One soul resided in the pupil of the eye and never left the body, even after death, so the Calusa would visit the buried and speak with the person. The other two souls were transferred to an animal. However, if the Calusa killed that animal, the soul would continue to be sent to a "lesser" animal until the soul ceased to exist.

Their ceremonies were dramatic, often including grand parades with priests and dancing women. The priests wore carved masks, described by the Spanish as "the shape of the devil, with some horns on their heads." The masks were then hung on the walls inside a temple.

---

4. Florida Center for Instructional Technology, 2002
5. Hann, 2003

The Spanish tried to convert the Calusa to Catholicism with little success. The Calusa's nobles' power depended on their religion: in Calusa culture, the king and his relatives were between gods and humans. A new, strange religion would have undermined and dismantled their authority over their people. The Calusa resisted the attempted conversions for almost 200 years.

What Happened to these Groups?

When the Spanish arrived in Florida 1513, there were between 100,000 and 300,000 indigenous peoples living in the area. This number would be decimated in under 200 years.

European Influence

The missions in northern Florida and southeastern Georgia were divided into four main sects based on the dialects among the Native Americans: the Apalachee, the Timucua, the Mocama, and the Guale.

Most Spanish explorers wanted to convert the Native Americans to Catholicism. In 1549, Father Luis de Cancer and three others visited Tampa Bay during the first true missionary effort in the Spanish territory of *La Florida*. However, the mission only lasted six weeks after de Cancer was killed by a native tribe, which scared many members of the Dominican missionary away from their efforts.

The Spanish missions in Florida started with the foundation of St. Augustine, and between 1565 and 1567, 10 missions, or presidos, were created from Port Royal Sound to Tampa Bay to stop other Europeans from establishing their own missions in the area. Most of these presidos did not last long — by 1573 the only remaining presido was St. Augustine and Santa Elena, which was abandoned in 1587.

The missions were short-lived for many reasons. They were first staffed by the Jesuits, an order of Roman Catholics, but after the murders of several missionaries, the Jesuits withdrew in fear from La Florida in 1572. This left only one other order, the Franciscan friars, to convert the Native Americans. The friars attempted to expand their goal westward, but their efforts collapsed in the 18th century when raids conducted by British soldiers depleted the resources and remaining missionaries in La Florida. Most of the Spanish missions were wiped out during the Apalachee massacre — a series of raids by the British and Native Americans from the Province of Carolina in 1704.

In retaliation and newfound efforts to expand Spanish influence in the area, the Spanish took many natives as slaves and killed those who resisted their expeditions. Between the wars and the new diseases ravaging the native populations, large areas of Florida were left mostly uninhabited by the early 1700s.

Sickness

Indigenous people like the Timucua and Calusa had never been exposed to the germs European explorers had brought to the new world aboard their ships and domesticated animals. They contracted never-before-seen Western sicknesses, and their immune systems often could not handle the new diseases, killing off much of the native population.

These foreign, fatal diseases included the bubonic plague, pneumonic plague, chicken pox, diphtheria, cholera, influenza, scarlet fever, smallpox, typhus, tuberculosis, measles, and whooping cough. Such diseases are something called crowd diseases; people who have contracted the disease and survived will from then on be immune to it. As a result, in the midst of a smaller a population than found in Europe, the disease eventually dies out.

For example, the measles disease needs a constant supply of about 300,000 non-immune people in order for the disease to survive. If the population size of people that can be infected falls below this number, the virus will cause sickness and death, but become extinct after one epidemic. In Native American populations, the measles would wreak havoc, the population numbers would drop, and the disease would become extinct. Once the population recovered, creating a new generation, the disease could return and the cycle would repeat itself.

Hundreds of thousands of Native Americans died of European diseases within the first 200 years of European contact. Smallpox killed the most, along with measles, influenza, and the bubonic plague.

The Native American's healing methods were rarely effective against the European diseases. In fact, they often made them worse. Native tribes often used sweat baths to treat illnesses, but the steamy water actually increased mortality in diseases like smallpox and measles which brought fever to the afflicted.

When the customary healing methods failed to work, the natives began to lose faith in their traditional religions. This gave the seemingly-immune Christian missionaries an opportunity to spread their influence. The natives saw that the Christians did not die from disease and felt that it must be because of their more powerful religion. So while the Europeans' disease killed many, those indigenous people turned to the same Christians who made them ill as the members of a better faith than their own.

Chapter 2
European Invasion!

> "Then the hard, dry Spaniards came exploring through, greedy and realistic, and their greed was for gold or God. They collected souls as they collected jewels. They gathered mountains and valleys, rivers and whole horizons, the way a man might now gain tittle to building lots."
> — John Steinbeck, *East of Eden*

The year was 1492, and Christopher Columbus had sailed the ocean blue, wreaking havoc wherever he and his ships landed. His explorations were celebrated in Spain and set off waves of exploration to the Americas that stretched all the way to Peru.

The Spanish were excited about the prospect of gold in the "New World," and the search for riches, fame, and glory meant that thousands of poor people enlisted in the Spanish military for a chance to share in the wealth. In Spanish culture, the eldest son inherited all the of the father's wealth — meaning that the younger siblings often had to find glory and money elsewhere. Those younger siblings of Spain often joined the exploration to the Americas to look for gold and seek their fortune. These adventurers were called the conquistadors.

Juan Ponce De León

Widely credited as being one of the first Westerners to reach Florida, Juan Ponce de León was an explorer and Spanish conquistador. He had sailed with Christopher Columbus and became a governor of Puerto Rico, but lost his title after Columbus' son challenged him for the position. As a consolation prize, the king of Spain gave Ponce de León a charter, or a grant, to go look for new lands. Ponce de León accepted.

Juan Ponce De León.

He took three ships — the Santiago, the San Cristobal, and the Santa Maria de la Consolacion — with around 200 men and left Puerto Rico on March 4, 1513. The crew sailed along the Bahamas (then known as the Lucayos) and found an "undiscovered" island on March 27, Easter Sunday. Some historians think that this "island" was really the peninsula of Florida. Others believe that the island was another northern Bahaman island.

In any case, the fleet sailed on the Atlantic until April 2, when they spotted more land. Ponce De León named the new mass La Florida because the landscape was very green and because it was the Easter season, or Pascua Florida (Festival of Flowers). Although Palm Sunday had already passed by then, he called the separated Florida Keys "The Martyrs" because they reminded him of the Christians who had been beheaded for their faith.

No one knows where Ponce De León originally landed, and the precise location has been debated among historians for many years. Some think he landed at St. Augustine; others think it was at a small harbor now named Ponce De León Inlet. Most historians agree that he and his crew landed around Melbourne Beach, although there is not much proof to confirm the theory.

Ponce De León sailed south along the shoreline, meeting the Timucua, Tequesta, and Calusa peoples. These tribes were not friendly, viewing Ponce De León as a danger, but a danger that brought them the tools like the guns that they so desperately wanted. The first gunshot by a white man in Florida (and the entire United States) occurred when a group of native men tried to steal a Spanish boat. De León himself fired the shot — the first act of a war against the native tribes that would not officially end until the 19th century.

After a two months' exploration, Ponce De León rounded Cape Florida and headed up to the Gulf of Mexico. There they were met with more hostility from the tribes, and after an attack by Native Americans in war canoes, the Spanish crew fled the area. They traveled back to Spain without establishing any settlements in Florida.

While the expedition was technically a failure, the Spanish king mostly wanted gold, and Ponce De León's venture provided him with 5,000 gold pesos from Puerto Rico. The Spanish had also learned something invaluable: Florida was not a place to get rich quick.

Ponce De León would probably have never traveled back to Florida if Hernan Cortes had not made his fortune in Mexico. To Ponce De León, Cortes' success meant hidden wealth *was* to be found in the Americas — he would just have to look harder for it. The conquistador set sail once more around 1521, determined to be successful and conquer Florida, once and for all.

Unfortunately for him, this final quest would ultimately be his downfall.

When his ship finally arrived in Florida, he landed on the familiar Gulf coast upon which he'd first set foot eight years ago. Things hadn't changed much, and Ponce de León was again attacked by Calusa warriors who shot arrows made of sharpened fish bones. One of those arrows struck his thigh.

In today's world, the injury would be easily treatable. But Ponce de León lived in a time in which the miracles of modern medicine were merely a fantasy, and infection soon took over. Ponce de León was evacuated to Cuba, where he died slowly of gangrene and fever in July 1521.

The Fountain of Youth

In addition to gold and glory, there may have been another reason Ponce de León was exploring Florida. According to one popular legend, the explorer was searching for the mystical Fountain of Youth: a legendary natural water spring that supposedly renewed the youth of anyone who bathed in it or drank from it. The legend of the fountain has been told across the world for years, appearing as early as 5th century B.C. Stories of similar fountains have been found among the natives of the Caribbean during the early 16th century.

Though knowledge of the Fountain of Youth spread across the world long before Ponce de León landed in Florida, the stories of his quest for the eternal fountain did not become known until after his death. Author Gonzalo Fernández de Oviedo y Valdés wrote in 1535 that Ponce de León was searching for the magical waters of Bemini to stop aging; in 1575, Hernando de Escalante Fontaneda, who had lived among the natives of Florida for 17 years following a shipwreck, published his memoir. Within it, he wrote that Ponce de León supposedly searched for the Fountain of Youth there. However, most historians believe that de León's quest for gold and Spanish conquest far outweighed any real consideration of a magical fountain.

Though never proven, the Fountain of Youth myth may be based on fact; some say the fountain symbolized the Bahamian "love vine," which was brewed by locals as a love potion. Ponce de León might have been looking for the vine as another way to make money.

Today, the Fountain of Youth Archaeological Park in St. Augustine is a memorial to the area where Ponce de León supposedly landed. The property was a tourist attraction as early as the 1870s, when a St. Augustine real estate promoter named John Whitney bought some land with a small spring, naming it "Ponce de León Spring," equating it with the Fountain of Youth. He sold tourists water and tried to sell them the land.

Luella Day McConnell created the modern-day tourist attraction in 1904. Legend says that Dr. McConnell used diamonds and cash from the Klondike Gold Rush of 1898 to purchase the park property from Mr. H.H. Williams, earning her the nickname "Diamond Lil." It is also said that Dr. McConnell received the nickname because she had a diamond in her front tooth.

In 1908, she sailed for Spain, searching for proof that her property was truly the site of the Fountain of Youth. When she arrived back in Florida, she "discovered" a cross that she claimed to have been hidden behind a tree. She said that she found a box with a salt holder given to Ponce de León by Christopher Columbus and a piece of paper that supposedly chronicled Ponce de León's landing in St Augustine.

Of course, she had planted the evidence, but it worked. Tourists soon visited the area to drink water and buy the souvenirs. Dr. McConnell died in 1923 in a car accident, and the property passed to her manager, Walter Fraser. He turned her creation into one of Florida's biggest tourist attractions, claiming legitimacy. He even threatened to sue those who publicly doubted its authenticity.

The Smithsonian Institution performed the first archaeological digs at the "Fountain of Youth" in 1934. Archaeologists found a large number of Christianized Timucua burials, pointing the park as the location of the first Christian Mission in the United States. Later, the park was confirmed as the oldest inhabited European settlement in North America. The park now has both native and colonial artifacts on exhibit to celebrate St. Augustine's Native American and European heritage.

Hernando De Soto

Ponce de León may have been the first European explorer to set foot on Florida, but he certainly was not the last. Another member of the "Florida Explorer Hall of Fame" is conquistador Hernando De Soto.

De Soto had made a name for himself in the Central American slave trade, helping the conquistadors take over Peru in 1532. De Soto asked for permission from Spanish King Carlos V to become a conquistador in South America, but he was instead given ownership of La Florida. He was given the titles of adelantado, or captain general, and governor over any 200 leagues of coast that he could "conquer, pacify, and populate." He was also made the governor of Cuba, and set sail for his new countries on April 7, 1538.

Hernando De Soto.

In May 1539, de Soto and his crew landed in an area generally thought to now be south Tampa Bay. The crew was huge and included more than 600 soldiers, 12 priests, women, servants, slaves, 223 horses, mules, dogs, and a herd of pigs.

De Soto named the land Espíritu Santo, or Holy Spirit. Near his port, the group discovered a Spanish man, Juan Ortiz, living with the Mocoso tribe. He had learned the Timucua language while living in captivity and became an interpreter for de Soto.

Ortiz created a unique method for guiding de Soto's expedition and communication with the tribes, who spoke many dialects and languages. He established a method of communication in which a guide from each tribe who lived closely enough to the boundaries of another tribal area so as to know the other tribe's language could pass information and language to another guide from a different area, and so on, like a game of telephone for interpretation. De Soto trusted Ortiz, but many other members of the Spanish fleet did not. Ortiz and his methods were helpful to the Spanish, but he did not feel comfortable among his own countrymen anymore. After so many years of living among the natives, Ortiz was now accustomed to life with the tribes and refused to dress like a normal Spaniard.

For four years, De Soto and his men traveled across the region to what is now the southeastern United States. During this expedition, the Spanish claimed land that ran from Washington D.C. and west of the Mississippi, all the way to the tip of Florida. However, the expedition was not considered successful. After 3,700 miles of travel in the New World, only 311 survivors returned to Spain. All of the animals were dead; they had found none of the riches they expected; the only gems they could find were poor-quality pearls, and even those were lost in a fire; and they had failed to create a permanent settlement or spread Catholicism among the natives. In Florida, they had found only war, disease, and death.

Their exploration had diminished the native populations so much so that dozens of chiefdoms fell into decline or collapsed completely. The introduction of European germs to the natives of La Florida was devastating. The Native Americans were never before exposed to common European diseases, and therefore had no immunity to illnesses like smallpox, measles, or typhoid fever, and the plagues rapidly destroyed their population.

Remember the herd of pigs that de Soto and his crew brought to North America? Some of those pigs escaped and became feral. Their descendants are still found in the southwestern United States and are known as razorback pigs.

Sacre Bleu

Although Spain realized that conquering Florida was technically a waste of money, they still wanted to hold onto the land. When the French arrived on the peninsula later in the 16th century, a rivalry began between the two countries that would last many years.

Captain Jean Ribaut was chosen by his commanding officer to create a French colony and began the expedition with 150 colonists. His crew landed near St. Augustine in the spring of 1562, erecting a marble column with the French coat-of-arms near the St. Johns River, or what is now modern-day Jacksonville. He named it the "River May," after the month in which he found it, continued north, and established a settlement in South Carolina called "Charlesfort," after the French king. Then, Ribault set sail for Europe, leaving behind 27 members of his crew.

When Ribault returned to Europe, he found that a brutal war had broken out in France between Protestants and Catholics. Fleeing the country, he was arrested in England as a spy and imprisoned in the Tower of London. Between his detainment and France's political troubles, they were not able to send any more reinforcements to the settlement at Charlesfort until 1564.

After the Spanish heard about the French colony on "their" land, they were furious. Philip II licensed Lucas Vaqquez de Ayllon the younger to visit Florida, but he never left. The Cuban governor sent a group to explore the French base, but they found it deserted.

Meanwhile, the French had already sent another explorer to colonize Florida. Rene de Laudonniere was more prepared than de Ayllon and brought livestock and tools. There were women, children, artisans and nobles, but not enough soldiers. Jean Ribaut returned to try and save the settlement after he was released from jail. Once he arrived, the French built Fort Caroline around the St. Johns River in Florida as a safe haven for Protestant refugees who were religiously persecuted, and set out to explore what they called "New France."

This period of exploration did not last long, though. As was the case with many expeditions in the New World, relations with the Native American tribes like the Timucuans soon soured, and the colony began to starve. Supplies soon ran out, and the colonists became desperate, some even rebelling. In December 1564, 70 men captured de Laudonniere and forced him to authorize their departure. Those men left for the Caribbean in search of treasure, but instead were captured by the Spanish.

The Spanish king, Phillip II, now realized the French threat was greater than ever before. The race to keep Florida under Spanish control began.

Fighting with the French and Spanish

King Phillip II of Spain knew he had to do something to maintain control over the Florida territory, and granted a new charter to a Florida adelantado, Pedro Menéndez de Aviles. Menéndez was promised the offices of both governor and captain general so long as he founded two cities and converted all the natives to the Roman Catholic faith. If he succeeded, Menéndez would receive a land grant and the title of marquis.

Menéndez believed that Florida ultimately held the key to riches and a route to the Orient, and told the king:

> If the French or British should come to settle Florida . . .
> it would be the greatest inconvenience, as much for the
> mines and territories of New Spain as for the navigation
> and trade of China and Molucca, if that arm of the sea
> goes to the South Sea, as it is certain . . . By being masters
> of Newfoundland . . . Your Majesty may proceed to master
> that land . . . It is such great land and [situated] at such a
> good juncture, that if some other nations go to settle it . . .
> it will afterwards be most difficult to take and master it.[6]

Menéndez believed and hoped that Florida could be profitable for himself
and for Spain and thought agriculture, livestock, fisheries, and the forests
would be plentiful in the region. He also believed there were water passages
that connected with the mines of New Spain and the Pacific and some that
crossed Florida from the Atlantic to the Gulf of Mexico.

In June 1565, Menéndez and a crew of a thousand men sailed for Florida,
arriving at Cape Canaveral. Spain knew that Jean Ribaut of France, who
had returned to Florida, was already living somewhere on the peninsula
with reinforcements, and Menéndez found them docked off the St. Johns
River. After a quick battle, the French retreated to the sea, and Menéndez
sailed south.

Menéndez took "formal possession" of all of Florida when he finally landed
on August 28, 1565, which was the feast day of St. Augustine of Hippo. He
named the colony San Agustin, placing the land and its inhabitants under
the rule of King Phillip II. This meant Menéndez could legally give land to
his followers and make treaties with the Native Americans. He and his crew
built the first fort in Florida around a longhouse given to him by a member
of the Eastern Timucua people.

---

6. Menedez, 1565

The French later attempted to attack the new settlement but failed. When a storm hit the French fleet, leaving the French colony, Fort Caroline, wide open, Menéndez took his chance and attacked the settlement on September 20. He and his men killed most of the population, taking the women and children as prisoners. Only a small group of French survived the storm, and when they stumbled upon an inlet close to St. Augustine, Menéndez persuaded most of them — including Jean Ribaut — to surrender.

He then had them executed, sparing only young boys and those who claimed to be Catholic. This inlet is now known as Matanzas, or "place of slaughter," and serves as a reminder of the violence of Spain and its colonizing efforts in the Florida region. After capturing Fort Caroline and killing his prisoners, Menéndez hung their bodies on trees with the words, "Not as Frenchmen but as Lutherans." The murders upset both Protestant and Catholic French, and the king of France sent complaints to the Spanish court, but instead of being punished for the killing, Menéndez and his crew received honors from Phillip II.

The French wanted revenge. Dominique (or Domingue) de Gourgue, a French nobleman and soldier, was infuriated by Spain's actions. During a war, he had been captured by the Spanish and spent time in their prisons in 1557. He was determined to avenge his fallen Frenchmen, though they were Protestants, and he was a Catholic. He sold everything he owned and borrowed money from his brother to recruit a crew and take command of three ships. De Gourge sailed to Cuba with 200 men, never telling them of the real reason for their expedition until they arrived in the New World. Once there, he told his men of his true plan of revenge and they agreed to help. They left Cuba to attack the Spanish at the old Fort Caroline, which had been renamed Fort San Mateo, and enlisted some of the French's old native allies. The fort was soon surrendered to the French.

The French and Native Americans killed the surviving Spanish as retribution for Fort Caroline and other massacres of Protestants, hanging the prisoners with the words, "Not as Spaniards but as murderers." The Spanish rebuilt the fort but permanently abandoned the structure the next year.

Though the French wished to dislodge the Spanish from Florida, they were unable to create much of an upset. Their raids on St. Augustine never harmed the city, so the Spanish remained in control. Razing the remnants of the French's Charlesfort, the Spanish established Santa Elena, declaring it the capital of La Florida until its eventual abandonment in 1587.

The first European and African babies born in the United States were both born in Florida. The first recorded birth was in Saint Augustine in 1566 and was the first birth of a child of European ancestry in the continental United States. The first recorded birth of a black child in the continental United States was listed in 1606, 13 years before enslaved Africans were brought to Jamestown in 1619.

With the French now safely out of the way, Menéndez turned his attention to colonizing the rest of the peninsula for the Spanish crown. His efforts were mostly successful, and for most of the next 200 years, Spain controlled La Florida.

Settling the Land

In 1569, ships with Spanish farmers, their wives, and their children landed in St. Augustine. There were 273 people in all; 193 of them were sent on to Santa Elena to settle the land. Once there, the settlers built houses, worked the lands, raised livestock, traded, and started city governments. By October of that same year, 327 people lived in Santa Elena, including the settlers and soldiers. The Hispanic culture and traditions that those settlers and soldiers had observed in Europe traveled all the way across the Atlantic Ocean and were infused into their New World lives.

Menéndez had specifically recruited farmers, promising them wealth and success in Florida. He said he would:

> give them their passage and pay for their freight. Having arrived at this land, I will give them lands and estates for their farms and stockraising, and within two years a dozen cows with one bull, two oxen for plowing, 12 sheep, and the same number of goats, hogs and chickens, and two mares and one farmhand, and a house constructed, with its winepress and a male and female slave and vineshoots to plant. I do not have the capability to do this, but I believe that there will be merchants who, once they know how good this land is for cultivation . . . might wish to put in a part of their wealth in that profitable agricultural enterprise — in order to settle themselves on large haciendas of sugar mills, livestock and farms of bread and wine.[7]

The farmers who agreed to settle Florida came from the Iberian peninsula, a small section of land between Spain and Portugal. They were mostly small farmers, or labradores, and most raised sheep, hogs, donkeys, mules, and horses to serve as work animals. They had gardens and orchards and grew crops like wheat, grapes, and olives. However, the climate in that area was harsh and water was scarce. Those who moved to Florida hoped to find lush, rich lands that would sustain their crops. Many learned to plant new crops, like corn, which wasn't found in Spain; it soon replaced wheat as the Hispanic carbohydrate. Sugar wasn't grown in Florida, but woods like ju-

7. Menéndez, 1566

niper, oak, and laurel were used for medicine, as well as sassafras root bark. The settlers also began trading furs with the Native Americans.

The culture in La Florida echoed Spain's own customs at the time, while also beginning to develop its own. St. Augustine and Santa Elena were both vibrant areas, operating like many European cities. Peddlers, blacksmiths, carpenters, and taverns were common in the Florida cities along with fishermen and hunters. There were even boardinghouses for unmarried men. The Spanish settlements were also hierarchal societies — ordinary people had few possessions of any sort, while nobles like Menéndez lived like royalty with ornate rugs, wall hangings, fancy linens, and elegant clothing. The settlers kept to their homeland's religion easily, building the Tridentine Roman Catholic Church for worship. The Floridian church dominated their life — the church bells even narrated the hours and days, just like they did in Spain.[8]

Life in the New World wasn't perfect, though. There were issues with government, and although the average Spanish immigrant had adapted to life in Florida, surviving in the tropics was still not easy. One man summed up his experience like this:

> I have suffered hunger, nudity and much misery, not because the land is so bad as they hold it to be, but due to the poor government it has had, and because their resources were little to conquer so many people and such a great land.[9]

8. Gannon, 1996
9. Martínez, 1577

Slaves in Florida — Fort Mose

Along with the government, church, and crops, the Spanish brought another source of income to the region: slaves.

Ponce de León brought the first African slaves to La Florida in 1513. The Spanish attempted to settle in Georgia with slaves, but when that experiment proved disastrous, most fled to the Caribbean. Some conquistadors like de Soto had also taken Native Americans as slaves in addition to their African slaves.

When Pedro Menéndez arrived, he brought 48 African slaves to St. Augustine. While some escaped to live with the Native Americans, many stayed and began to integrate with the Spanish population.

The Spanish culture of slavery, while still cruel, was different than the more well-known British version of slavery. The Spanish government officially recognized slaves as humans with certain rights and privileges. Slaves had the right to sue their owners if they were mistreated and could petition the king. In fact, during this time, the Spanish granted any escaped British slave their rights as long as they converted to Catholicism and served four years in the Spanish militia.

This was not out of the kindness of their hearts, though. The Spanish wanted to destabilize the British presence in Florida by seeming like an appealing option to slaves seeking refuge from British ownership. If the slaves of the British all fled to Florida, certainly the British colonies would fail. In addition to this underhanded scheme, Spain also created a settlement that would exist on the front-lines against attacks from the British: Fort Mose.

In 1738, Governor Manuel de Montiano and his men began building the Gracia Real de Santa Teresa de Mosé military fort, about two miles north of

St. Augustine. Slaves who had escaped from the British were placed at the fort and recognized as free. The able-bodied former slaves were inspected and enrolled in the Spanish militia. That was how Fort Mose, the first free African-American settlement legally sanctioned in what would become the United States, was begun. The village of about 100 permanent residents had a wall around it, with houses, a church, and a fort within.

In 1740, the British attacked and captured the fort in the Siege of Fort Mose. A Spanish force made up of Spanish troops, Native Americans, and a free, black militia counterattacked and eventually defeated the British but destroyed the fort in the process. The inhabitants of Fort Mose resettled in St. Augustine.

There, many earned a living by working on projects for the government or by becoming members of a ship's crew. They helped to trap escaped prisoners, forage for food, and round up wild cattle and horses in the spring. Although technically free men, they were still at the bottom of the social order and considered threats by poorer whites. By 1752, the Spanish had rebuilt Fort Mose and forced most free blacks to return to the fort, although they had grown used to life in the city of St. Augustine.

The new Fort Mose had 22 structures, including homes, a church, and a house built for the Franciscan priests. There were 67 people listed as living there in the 1759 census. Those who lived in Mose spoke several languages, including Spanish, various Native American dialects, languages from West Africa, and other European languages.

Once the British took over East Florida in 1763, Fort Mose was abandoned. Most of the free black population left for Cuba with the Spanish settlers. At that time, there were around 3,000 blacks living around St. Augustine and Fort Mose, about one-quarter of whom were free.

Today, Fort Mose is a U.S. National Historic Landmark and a Historical State Park. It is considered the "premier site on the Florida Black Heritage Trail." The National Park Service (NPS) notes the site as a predecessor of the Underground Railroad, through which many slaves escaped to freedom before the American Civil War. Although most slaves used the Underground Railroad to escape to the North and Canada, some went through Florida on their way to live in the Bahamas and Mexico.

In 1986, an archaeological dig discovered the original Fort Mose, as well as the second facility that was built in 1752. The museum on the site displays interpretive panels illustrating the history of the site; replicas of a chose, or cooking hut; a garden; and a Spanish boat known as a barca chata.

The Fort Mose Historic State Park boardwalk leading from the observation area.

 Pirates of the Caribbean isn't just a Disney ride and movie — there were *real* pirates sailing along the coast of Florida looking for treasure. One of these pirates, Black Caesar, supposedly buried his treasure on Elliot, an island in the Florida Keys.

The Spanish in Power

As Spain once again took control of Florida, the mission to convert Native Americans to Catholicism began to spread across the peninsula. Jesuits were sent as missionaries to Florida to convert the "Indios" and Menéndez himself planned to establish order between the various native tribes, expel what the Church considered heathenism and heresy, and spread the gospel of Jesus Christ. He signed treaties with a few Native Americans tribes like the Calusa and began to trade items with them like furs and corn.

The Franciscan friars charged with converting the Native Americans took their missions to the source, placing crosses in town squares, giving the chiefs gifts, and preaching to the tribes about Christianity. Churches and convents began to sprout up in Native American towns, giving the natives access to exotic, European goods and new tools like guns.

The Spanish also inserted themselves into the Sabana System — the natives' method of public finance. According to custom, the members of a Native American town planted a sabana, or field, of maize for their chief, and then another sabana for the communities. With the arrival of the settlers, the Native Americans were told to clear and plant other sabanas for the king and the convent. They were also pressured to sell their harvest to the presido. As a reward, the chiefs of the Native Americans were given gifts of European clothes, weapons, cloth, beads, and tools.

From 1587 on through the 1620s, the Spanish created mission provinces along the east coast of Florida and up through the St. Johns River. There were two districts: the Mocamo (Saltwater) and the Agua Dulce (Freshwater), and the entire expansion was known as the Nearer Pacifications.

Many Native Americans did not give up their cultures entirely nor submit to Spanish rule easily. Some tribes revolted and fought against the Spanish, often with French or British aid. A famous revolt that would last for six years, known as the Guale Uprising of 1597, began with the killing of five Spanish friars.

There was also the looming presence of other countries' claims to the region to consider. Menéndez built four forts from Florida to South Carolina to guard the Spanish treasure ships and colonies.

Although Spain had found wealth in the "New World" due to gold and silver being found in abundance, as well as the newly established island sugar and rice farms, Florida was ultimately a money pit. The land itself was poor in minerals, and the soil practically untillable. It was difficult to grow crops along the shore, and those that could be grown inland competed with other crops that the Spanish grew back home. All in all, Florida was a financial burden on Spain. Menéndez was a decent governor of the peninsula, but he tired of it quickly, finding no fame or glory in Florida.

In fact, Florida was the only Spanish colony that didn't show a true profit. The wealthier colonies and their settlements supported Florida, but the money came late. The payment, or situado, only came once a year via a situado ship. The ship gave the Floridian settlement the hard currency needed to pay those who worked in government or for the church, as well as for food and drink.

 Visiting St. Augustine? Try to find Treasury Street, the narrowest street in the United States — it's only seven feet wide. The street was connected to the Royal Spanish Treasury and was deliberately made to be narrow to prevent thieves from escaping with gold from the building.

The British are Coming!

In 1586, the British attacked Florida.

Spain and the British Empire were already at war back in Europe: King Phillip II was furious after Queen Elizabeth I of England announced her support of the Protestant Dutch rebels who had revolted against the Roman Catholic king. Aware of his fury, the queen ordered Sir Francis Drake to attack the Spanish New World in a preventative strike.

Drake and the British landed in Florida to find the city of St. Augustine totally deserted but were soon surprised by an ambush. The Spanish lied in wait beyond the outskirts of the settlement's fort and opened fire but were unable to defeat the British and had to beat a hasty retreat. Drake and his men were then in total control of the settlement and burned St. Augustine to the ground. The buildings were torched, the crops were destroyed, and anything of value was taken for profit or destroyed. The San Juan fort was also burned, and any artillery was carried away by the invaders.

After the British left, Menéndez and the Spanish returned and found the ruins of St. Augustine. Nearly everything had been destroyed. Receiving aid from the Spanish-occupied Cuba, the fort was replaced by the present-day Castillo de San Marcos.

Sir Francis Drake and his forces destroyed nearly all of St. Augustine — which would be rebuilt nine times over while under Spanish control — leading Spain to build the huge Fort San Marcos, constructed with a mixture of shells called coquina. This attack on St. Augustine would signify another new era in Spanish rule: the constantly looming threat of the imposing British Empire.

When Drake returned to England, he was hailed as a national hero. In Spain, however, the news was devastating. Rumors that the British used a settlement in the North for piracy alarmed the Spanish, although they could never find it. Fearing another raid, the Spanish abandoned Santa Elena, effectively ending the Spanish presence in modern-day South Carolina.

When the British defeated the Spanish Armada in a 1588 massive sea battle, Spanish control over the New World began to decline. Once the English colony in Jamestown was established in 1607, the British threat to the Spanish hold on the New World became real. Although the Jamestown colony nearly starved to death their first year in America, they survived and their colonies spread south, shrinking Spanish control even further.

When the British began to settle South Carolina in 1658, Florida became a bigger target. St. Augustine was attacked again in 1665 and 1668. The number of Spanish Jesuits and missionaries in the area began to fall. In 1655, Spain had 70 missionaries and claimed to convert 20,000 Native Americans. Only 50 years later, there were only 12 missionaries and 400 sympathetic Native Americans. Worse yet, the British burned Spanish missions in northern Florida and executed any Native Americans in league with the Spanish. This collapse of the Spanish mission system opened Florida up for slave raids: the English would capture and sell Native Americans into slavery, both on the continent and on the English plantations in the Caribbean.

Once the French and Indian War began, Florida was considered a true battleground — the French even captured Pensacola, formerly a Spanish settlement. Inch by inch, Spain was losing its hold on Florida. The question was . . . who would take it over?

The French and Indian War

The impending influence of the British Empire extended beyond Florida's shores; the rivalry between the French and British was known worldwide. They were two very powerful countries and had conquered their fair share of territories, expanding their power throughout many continents. Finally, in 1754, the tension between the world powers broke, and the worldwide Seven Years' War began. Though there were skirmishes all across the world in this time, the war most well-known in the United States was the French and Indian War.

The British American and New France colonies were both supported by supplemental military units from their parent countries. At the start of the war, the French colonies had around 60,000 settlers across the North American continent; the British had nearly 2 million. To compensate for their vastly inadequate quantity of soldiers, the French began working with the Native Americans to defeat the formidable British army.

Though much of the fighting actually took place in the northern-most settlements in America, when Great Britain won the war, Spain was finally forced to give up Florida. In 1763, the Treaty of Paris was signed by Spain, France, and Great Britain, officially ending the French and Indian War. As a condition of the treaty, France gave up almost all its land in North America to the British, and Spain exchanged Florida for the formerly British-held Cuba.

The British separated Florida into two territories: East Florida and West Florida. Thus began the British Period during which the Union Jack flew over the peninsula.

Britain takes over

Although the British Empire knew Florida had been a financial drain on Spain, they still wanted control of the region.

They already had plenty of colonists in the northern colonies and realized that they could lure them south with potential trading opportunities. The British also thought that they could perhaps repair relations with the Native Americans by tempting settlers to leave native lands in the west and come settle in Florida instead. They began advertising Floridian land to entice settlers to move there, even offering British soldiers from the French and Indian War special grants. To further recruit those from the South, slavery would be allowed in the new colony.

St. Augustine was designated as the capital of East Florida, while Pensacola became the capital of West Florida. This new arrangement meant that the British could rule over the region without having to sail around the enormous Florida Keys. The Floridians were appointed a governor, a lieutenant governor, and a chief justice to manage the executive branch, and a council served as the colony's upper house, or congress.[10] And in keeping with the religious climate of the homeland, the Church of England replaced the Catholic Church as the official religion in Florida.

Trade among the British colonies began according to the various regions of production and distribution. Tropical crops were sent to South Carolina while products like indigo dyes were sent north. Slaves were brought in for the large plantations. The Floridian economy began to adjust to the ex-

---

10. Pbchistory, n.d.

tensive norm of the British colonies. Some areas, like Pensacola struggled, producing nothing more than lumber and furs. Those who lived in the area survived on cheap crops like corn, beans, and rice.

British colonists poured into the region, bringing with them their British customs, but some influence from the Spanish remained. The Spanish who had long-occupied the area had evolved and transformed various aspects of their culture to best suit the unique Floridian needs, while the British were more accustomed to the temperate northern colonies. The Spanish coquina houses and courtyards of St. Augustine remained to keep out the harsh wind and the ravenous mosquitoes.

Slavery in Florida

Floridian leaders wanted efficient economic prosperity, and free labor — or slaves– was how they decided to accomplish that. Nearly all laborers in Florida at the time were enslaved men and women, most of whom had been kidnapped from African countries.

As the economy grew, so did the need for slaves. The British governor, James Grant, promised free land and government support to the South Carolina and Georgian plantation owners who brought their households and their slaves with them down to Florida to relocate. Grant himself started an indigo plantation, called Grant's Villa, which paid off all of Grant's expenses. His success would go on to encourage other wealthy landowners to move south.

Florida's economy depended on the slavery system to survive. The London merchant Richard Oswald forced African slaves from Sierra Leone to today's Ormond Beach, where 240 people were put to work against their will. James Penman came to East Florida in 1767 and established a 10,000 acre estate at what is now Daytona Beach. He would own around 188 slaves across six rural estates in Florida.

Some slaves were able to buy their freedom and live and work in cities like St. Augustine. Many of them created new lives for themselves and were able to live in relative peace, but Georgian slave owners often complained about the free slaves who lived in Florida. In 1790, Spain gave in to pressure from the United States government and removed Florida's religious sanctuary policy, which guaranteed freedom to all slaves who crossed the Floridian border. But those who had already escaped and taken refuge in Florida would remain free.

Although slaves could no longer claim freedom through religious sanctuary in Florida, they could still buy their freedom or be given their freedom through military service. Many joined the Spanish army and won their freedom by suppressing revolts in Haiti. Others fled to join Native American tribes, forming new social groups like the Seminoles.

White citizens who migrated to Florida especially felt threatened by the presence of free blacks. The homesteaders worried about the free blacks' alliance with the Native Americans and the "bad example" they set for slaves that lived on plantations. As more and more white settlers moved south, those free former-slaves left, fearing violent retaliation. Many left for Cuba; still others moved to Mexico.

Turnbull Colony

Governor Grant only wanted to import black slaves from Africa to supply the work-force. He was worried that white Europeans, who were often employed to perform unskilled labor, would be sickened by the heat and humidity of Florida and be less productive than the theoretically heat-resistant Africans. As a result of his beliefs, most laborers were African slaves. However, there was one major exception to this rule — the Turnbull Colony.[11]

---

11. Gannon, 1996

In 1764, the British Parliament designated £500 (British pounds) to culti-
vate crops in East Florida, giving land grants to citizens who were willing to
move there. Dr. Andrew Turnbull, a Scottish physician, talked his wealthy
friends in Britain into starting a new settlement in Eastern Florida. He
planned to employ Greeks as laborers because he thought they would be
accustomed to a hot climate. Turnbull also assumed that he would be easily
able to convince others to leave the Ottoman Empire, which, at the time,
dominated most of what is now Eastern Europe.

He created a settlement he named Smyrnea, located south of St. Augustine
at Mosquito Inlet (now present day New Smyrna Beach and Edgewater).
More than 100 black slaves were purchased to work at Smyrnea, but many
of the other laborers were European indentured servants. Turnbull, who
had worked in Smyrna, Turkey for years, developed three 20,000 acres of
plantations with those indentured servants and slaves. It was nearly three
times the size of the colony at Jamestown.

 An indentured servant is a person who worked for a
definite period of time, usually without pay — but in
exchange for free passage to a new country.

This scale of industry at the settlement was bigger than any other development in Florida, and Turnbull traveled to the Mediterranean again to
recruit more Greek and Italian laborers. The settlers eventually produced
luxury crops of high quality like indigo, hemp, and sugarcane for making
rum.

Turnbull had high hopes for Smyrnea, but the high rates of sickness and
death, lack of food, labor unrest, and funding shortages lead to the eventual collapse of the settlement in 1777. Those who had managed to survive

the high mortality rates and brutal labor conditions left and settled in what was known as the "Minorcan Quarter" of St. Augustine. They became fisherman, merchants, and laborers, and some of their descendants still live in the area.[12]

The American Revolution

By the mid-1700s, trouble was brewing in the Northern American colonies. A group of revolutionaries began a rebellion for their freedom from the British. They fought in skirmishes, dumped tea into the Boston Harbor to protest the rising taxes, and eventually declared independence from their mother country. These men and women were known as Patriots, and by 1775, the American Revolution had begun.

A painting of the Boston Tea Party, where revolutionaries dumped tea in the Boston Harbor, an event that led to the American Revolution.

12. Florida Memory Blog, 2014

Those who sided with the British were known as Loyalists and wanted the rebellion swiftly dealt with. Across the Atlantic, the British king seethed, but Patriots like George Washington and Thomas Jefferson had begun forming what is now considered the United States of America.

The rumble of unrest did not encompass all of the East Coast. Florida, a British colony as of 1763, stayed loyal to the British Empire. The taxes that had so infuriated the revolutionaries did not affect East and West Florida. Even the proclamation that all colonists had to give shelter, food, and liquor to British soldiers barely affected those living on the peninsula. In fact, in Florida, soldiers were welcome: between raids from the Native Americans, the Spanish, and the French, British colonists needed *more* members of the King's army.

Today, when you study the original colonies in the United States, you read about 13: Delaware, Pennsylvania, Massachusetts Bay Colony (or what is now Massachusetts), New Jersey, Georgia, Connecticut, Maryland, South Carolina, New Hampshire, Virginia, New York, North Carolina, and Rhode Island. Florida, although technically a British colony, is always omitted. This is because most Floridians remained loyal to the crown during the revolution.

The colony could have sent delegates to sign the Declaration of Independence in Philadelphia, Pennsylvania, but they declined. As the Revolutionary War began, Loyalists who were spread across the other colonies often sought refuge in the British-friendly Florida. St Augustine transformed into a giant prisoner of war camp for captured revolutionaries. In fact, on August 11, 1776, when news of the Declaration of Independence reached leaders in St. Augustine, they were so angry that they made dummies of John Hancock and Samuel Adams and hung them in trees, lighting them on fire.

The Revolutionaries did not forget Loyalist Florida. General George Washington (who would later become the first United States president) knew about the area's strategic significance to the British. He wrote more than 80 letters to the Continental Congress and his generals about the Florida colonies, and he authorized five attacks on East Florida from 1776 and 1780. Other countries noticed England's weakness and took advantage of it — as a result of a series of battles from 1779 to 1781, Spain managed to recapture West Florida from the British for themselves.[13]

In January 1783, British, Spanish, French, and American negotiators met in Paris to discuss a new treaty. The northern 13 American colonies were given their independence and officially became a new country. East and West Florida, however, were given back to the Spanish as a reward for helping the revolutionaries during the war. On July 12, 1784, Spanish Governor Vizente Manuel de Zéspedes, oversaw the change of flags from British to Spanish at St. Augustine. The British had only controlled the area for 20 years.

Although the British lost Florida, they did not abandon the Florida Loyalists who had supported them during the war. Many moved to other British colonies like the Bahamas or Jamaica. Others even traveled back to England.[14]

Home, Sweet Home — Spain Returns

By 1785, the Spanish were back in Florida. The British had taken their time leaving the colony, staying close to the newly-formed United States in the hopes that the young democracy would fail. As the years passed, it

13. Brotenmarkle, 2016
14. Gannon, 1996

became clear that the new country was there to stay, and the Spanish were able to reclaim their Floridian territory.

As the Spanish moved back into Florida, they again began to try and lure people to their colony. They offered tax breaks, land grants, and cash. The Spanish governor eventually stopped requiring settlers to be slave-owners and Catholic. In fact, by 1795, about 15 percent of Florida's population was Protestant.[15] The Franciscans wanted to return to the area and try again to convert the Native Americans, but there was no real attempt to restart the missions.

The changes in policy and promises of new land barely helped. Because of the border argument, Spain forbade trading with the United States, so crops like oranges and rice could not make money for farmers. Fur trapping helped the economy, but wasn't nearly enough to supplement Spanish Florida's growing population. The Spanish kept the British separation of East and West Florida, governing from the two capitals of Pensacola and St. Augustine. A dispute over borders between the new United States immediately soured relationships between the two countries.

The United States constantly clashed with Spain, who eventually closed the port of New Orleans to American ships, harming the United States' economy and resulting in threats of invasion. In 1795, the two sides agreed to negotiate, reducing demand for the American military to take control of Florida — but the threat remained.

Relations worsened in 1803 when the United States gained the Louisiana Territory from France. This acquisition meant that the United States had land separating Florida from Mexico, further muddling the contentious border lines. Some even claimed that the United States had somehow pur-

15. Gannon, 1996

chased Western Florida. Americans began to demand that the government buy Florida from the Spanish. And yet, Spain held onto their land.

Florida was becoming a nightmare for Spain. Pirates waited along the coasts for ships and criminals found the peninsula a safe haven. The bills were piling up, and the Spanish could barely make a profit from only fur trapping. The colony was becoming weaker and weaker. Some land-hungry citizens saw their chance, and began invading the territory, claiming land for themselves. Florida was a wilderness — the question was, who would tame it?[16]

Republic of West Florida

In 1810, a group of American and British settlers in Baton Rouge, Louisiana learned that the Spanish governor was preparing to attack them. They held several secret meetings (and three public ones) to make a plan, eventually attacking a Spanish garrison at Fort San Carlos in Baton Rouge and capturing part of Florida, establishing what they called the Republic of West Florida.

Fulwar Skipwith, a distant cousin of Thomas Jefferson, became the Republic's first and only governor. The city of St. Francisville became its capital. The republic's constitution, based on the new United States Constitution, also divided the government into three branches. Under their new constitution, the country was officially deemed "State of Florida."

There was even a marching song by the Republic of West Florida Army, which included these lyrics:

> West Floriday, that lovely nation,
> Free from king and tyranny,

---

16. Clark, 2014

Thru' the world shall be respected,
For her true love of Liberty.

Unfortunately for the settlement, the United States government refused to recognize the independence of the Republic of West Florida. On October 27, 1810, President James Madison announced that the United States would take possession of the Republic. In his eyes, Florida was technically a part of the Louisiana Purchase. This was controversial at the time — his declaration was done without the approval of Congress nor through negotiation with the Florida Republic or Spain, who still technically owned Florida.

Although the Republic of West Florida had been interested in becoming part of the United States, its citizens ultimately decided to become their own country. When Madison decided that the new settlement would become a U.S. territory whether they liked it or not, Governor Skipwith announced that he and his troops would "surround the Flag-Staff and die in its defense."

William C. C. Claiborne, the military governor of Orleans Territory, was tasked with taking possession of Florida. He entered the Republic with 300 troops and would not recognize the West Florida government. The military pressure was too much, and Skipwith and the West Floridians eventually conceded and became part of the United States.

The "Bonnie Blue Flag" was the national flag of the Republic of West Florida. Consisting of a rectangular blue field with a single white star (representing the new republic), it later became one of the many flags of Confederate soldiers during the Civil War.[17]

---

17. Explore Southern History, 2013

The "Bonnie Blue Flag," which originated as the national flag of the Republic of West Florida.

The United States moved closer and closer to the Spanish territory of Florida. By 1812, the United States had captured all the land between the Perdida and Mississippi Rivers, turning part of the area into the new Louisiana territory. In 1814, the United States occupied what is now Mobile, Alabama. Although the Spanish protested, there was little they could do about it.[18]

Americans of English and Scottish descent traveled to northern Florida from Georgia and South Carolina to settle. They were not technically allowed to enter the colony, but the Spanish couldn't control the border. These migrants and the British settlers who stayed in Florida began to be known as Florida Crackers. The term "Cracker" was used in Elizabethan times to describe someone who was constantly bragging about their accomplishments.

---

18. Davis, 2013

The Republic of East Florida

The United States wanted Florida land no matter what, and many tried to acquire it through less-than-legal means. This is how another group of Americans decided to form their own republic, this time on the eastern side of Florida.

In 1812, General George Mathews and Colonel John McKee were ordered by President James Madison to visit the Spanish governor and acquire East Florida. Their instructions from a secret act of Congress were simple: they were to take control of any part of the Florida territories possible.

McKee declined, but Matthews was up to the challenge. He could not acquire any land straightforwardly with the Spanish, so instead he schemed to form a group of rebels to overthrow the local government. He tried to make them angry about the Spanish and convince them that a revolt would improve their lives. This didn't work either, however. The locals were happy with the Spanish government and did not want to stage a revolution.

Instead, Mathews tried recruiting rebellion leaders from among the frontier inhabitants. Mostly tradesmen, wood-choppers, and boatmen from around St. Marys, Georgia, and some militiamen, the rebels were also encouraged by slave-holders who wanted to end Native Americans raids on their property. Mathews told their leaders that he had the full authorization of a United States government that was determined to take possession of East Florida. Mathews promised the rebels weapons and the total support of the U.S. military in order to get control of the Spanish fort at Fernandina. He also pledged to defend the territory once they gave it to the United States.

On March 14, 1812, around 250 to 350 so-called "Patriots of Amelia Island" gathered on the Florida side of the St. Mary's River. Under the supervision of General Mathews, they selected temporary officers. Two days later, nine American gunboats aimed their guns at the town of Fernandina, demanding that the Spanish surrender the town and the port. The Spanish agreed, and the town was given to the Patriots, who immediately surrendered it to General Mathews. This began a march across Florida that would bring destruction to its inhabitants.

The East Republic of Florida flag was designed by Colonel Ralph Isaacs and featured a blue soldier charging with his bayonet on a white field. Below was the Latin phrase Salus populi lex suprema, meaning "the safety of the people, the supreme law."

Slightly ahead of the American troops, the Patriots of Amelia Island moved toward St. Augustine. There they would take some land, raise their flag, and force the "local authority" to give the territory to the United States troops, who would then lower the Patriot Flag and raise the American flag. The Patriots were protected by the United States and faced no opposition. The two groups marched, camped, looked for food, and fought together.

Although Congress had initially given General Mathews the power to take Florida from the Spanish, they started to feel uneasy about his new army of "Patriots." When the U.S. government learned about the events in East Florida, they began to worry about going to war with Spain. Secretary of State James Monroe (who later became the fifth president of the United States) ordered the American troops to withdraw, instructing them to "restore back to the Spanish authorities Amelia Island and such other posts of East Florida as had been thus taken from them."[19] He fired General Mathews on May 9.

---

19. Monroe, 1812

A map of the East and West Public of Florida territories.

However, sending messages in the 1800s wasn't as easy as sending a text message today. It took months for Monroe's order to reach the troops in Florida. Throughout the summer and fall, the United States and Patriot forces destroyed many plantations and farms. They took anything they could find. They destroyed crops and buildings, killed livestock, and abducted slaves. One rancher never recovered from having 800 of his cows taken when the East Floridian army destroyed his farm. Judge Isaac Bronson said that "the whole inhabited part of the province was in a state of utter desolation ruin."[20] Many settlers, disgusted by the "Patriot War," left Florida, never to return. By May of 1813, many parts of the state had been completely destroyed.

---

20. Bronson, 1858

Finally, on May 6, 1813, the American flag was lowered at Fernandina, and the remaining troops crossed the St. Marys River to Georgia. They had finally listened to the U.S. government and given up their new lands. Spain once again regained control of the region.

But the Patriots of Amelia Island were not finished with the region just yet. One year later, a group of volunteers from Georgia snuck back into Florida and began building Fort Mitchell. The fort was southwest of St. Augustine and south of present-day Gainesville. The settlers met as a political body on January 25, 1814, and declared the area to be the "District of Elotchaway of the Republic of East Florida." Once again, President Madison refused to recognize their authority, destroying the hopes of the Patriots who had wished to become their own territory.

Madison still wanted Florida for the United States, but 1812 was an election year, and the constant skirmishes in East Florida were embarrassing for the United States. If he stood behind the "Patriots of Amelia Island," it would have hurt his political career. He could not recognize them, thanks to politics. Florida would have to wait.[21]

21. Cusick, 2007

Chapter 3

The United States Has Florida Fever

"Cause it's the early 19th century
We'll take the land back from the Indians
We'll take the land back from the French and Spanish
And other people in other European countries
And other countries too
And also other places
I'm pretty sure it's our land anyway."
— Bloody Bloody Andrew Jackson by Michael Friedman

Years passed. Between the growing pressure from the United States and their own weakening political presence in the territory, Spain was almost ready to give up Florida. They had survived nearly 200 years in the area, facing raids from Native Americans, the French, the British, and now, the United States. They had tried to convert the indigenous people with little success and had barely made any profit. For some, it felt worthless to try and hold on to a small part of a peninsula that was across an entire ocean from the Crown in the Mother country.

In 1819, Secretary of State John Quincy Adams — the son of former president John Adams, who would later become president himself — offered the Spanish a deal: if they relinquished Florida, they would receive a portion of U.S.-owned Texas. At first, the Spanish declined, but eventually accepted the deal two years later. Their colonial system had begun to collapse throughout both North and South America, anyway, so they decided to take what they could get.

Spain eventually sold Florida for $5 million, finally abandoning their colony there after hundreds of years. However, it took a few wars with new Native American tribes — and one Andrew Jackson — for Florida to finally belong to the new United States.

The Arrival of the Seminole People

As the United States and European countries fought for Florida land, a new Native American tribe began to form before their very eyes. This tribe was known as the Seminoles.

The Seminole tribe has one of the most unique and fascinating backgrounds of indigenous nations. They formed their own tribe after separating from other groups in the present-day southeastern United States. They were fierce warriors who were determined to stay free and caused three separate wars in the Floridian region. A headache for the United States government, the Seminole tribe's history and culture is vital to understanding Floridian history.

There is evidence that the Seminole people are descendants of multiple groups of Native Americans who lived in the southeastern United States. When the Spanish arrived in Florida, nearly 200,000 Seminole ancestors lived among hundreds of tribes throughout the peninsula.

However, true Seminole history started with the Creek tribe from Georgia and Alabama. They traveled to Florida in the 1700s after conflicts with Europeans and other tribes became too fierce. Some groups of Lower Creeks migrated to Florida to avoid confrontation with the Upper Creeks. Others were searching for better areas in which to grow corn and other crops.

The Creeks, who had moved away from tribes up north, began to form their own traditions and cultures. This is a process known as ethnogenesis — or "the formation and development of an ethnic group." Some were dark-skinned and known as the "Black Seminoles." They are the descendants of free blacks and escaped slaves who joined with Seminole groups in Spanish Florida.

As the native population became more involved in European trade, and as tensions between the English, French, Spanish, and Native Americans increased, what was left of the Creek society began to unravel. The leadership that passed between families did not work anymore; the chiefs were looking to make deals with whoever they could find.

In 1765, Governor James Grant from the British colonies called the remaining Creek leaders together for a meeting called the Picolata Congress, where he would try to gain land east of the St. Johns River for the British. One Creek, Cowkeeper, did not attend — and although he was considered Creek, he had very little to do with the other Creek leadership and often led raids against the Spanish. Cowkeeper's relationship with other Creeks and the European settlers illustrates how complicated it is to generalize the evolution from Creeks to the Seminoles. Eventually, Cowkeeper would establish his tribe as separate altogether — calling themselves the Seminoles.

The name "Seminole" comes from a Spanish word, "*cimarones*," or people that were separate from, or apart from, their ancestral populations. In the native Muskogean tongue, that word became "Seminole." Cimarron can also be linked to the English word maroon, which was used to describe the communities of runaway slaves in Florida.[22]

A photo of members of the Seminole tribe.

Once the British gave Florida back to the Spanish, there were few, if any, Creeks left. Now there were only Seminoles. In 1774, there were nine Seminole towns; by 1821, there were around 36. The Seminoles expanded so much due to their trade. They hunted deer, and sold or traded the products to Europeans — for 18 pounds of a skins, a hunter could get a new gun; for 60 pounds, they could get a saddle for their horse. Plantation agriculture developed; and corn, rice, watermelons, potatoes, peaches, and pumpkins were sold to residents in St. Augustine.

---

22. Seminole Tribe, n.d.

Early Seminole history can be split into two periods: the Colonization period (1716-1767), when Creek towns began to move into Florida, and the Enterprise period (1767-1821), during which they prospered under the British and Spanish of Florida.

Seminole Culture Forms

The Seminole culture has similarities with the Creek culture, but as the tribe began to expand and create its own traditions, it developed its own unique way of life. For example, as the Seminoles adapted to the Florida environment, they developed their own traditions like constructing thatched-roof houses known as 'chickees.' They spoke Mikasuki and Creek, both Muskogean languages.

Origins of the Creek and Seminole culture can be found in the tribes that lived in the lower Southeast. By the 10th century, Creek societies were divided into clans determined by the mother's family. The succession of chiefly power went from a man to his nephew.

The Creek religious beliefs were influenced by the four cardinal directions: east, west, north, and south. The east was associated with the rising sun, and thought to have beneficial power. Colors were symbolic — with red the color of war, and white associated with peace.

Creek religion stressed the idea of purity of both mind and body, achieved through using tobacco, the act of blood-letting (draining small amounts of blood), and drinking something known as the "black drink," which was brewed from holly leaves, to induce vomiting. Annual or seasonal ceremonies were held in the center of the villages and represented community purity. They held the Green Corn Dance, or busk (meaning to fast in the Creek language).

The Green Corn Dance was often held at the square grounds of each clan. The square grounds had four open pavilions at each side of the square. One of them was specifically designed for the chief.

The ceremony lasted four days and consisted of both social and solemn activities. Men and women would play games with webbed ball sticks; boys would become men through a naming ritual; crimes and grievances were heard on the "Court Day." There were circles of dancers, who moved gracefully in patterns across a ritually prepared low mound of earth. The dances were often connected to an animal spirit like the snake, alligator, and the crawfish. The Green Corn Dance is still practiced by the Seminoles today.

Creek traditional music includes rattles, hand drums, water drums, and flutes. Folk songs are used to treat the sick and wounded and to encourage animals to be hunted easily. Hunting songs are sung without instrumental accompaniment and through call-and-response. The Seminoles wanted to produce harmony and a sense of wellbeing within their community.

The men hunted and fought; the women tended to gardens, fished, and made pottery and clothing. Rewards for bravery included prestige among the warrior's peers, tattoos, and for the young adult, a chance to earn a warrior's name.[23]

First of Three: The Seminole Wars

When the Spanish arrived in the mid-16th century, the Creeks were able to avoid immediate extinction. Although they, too, suffered effects of new diseases and direct conflict with the Europeans, they lived in a hard-to-reach area and stayed relatively away from the new colonists.

---

23. Gannon, 1996

Andrew Jackson in Pensacola during the First Seminole War.

However, as the British took over the area, the Georgian Creeks began trading animal skins and quickly created an economic partnership. The Creeks even attacked Spanish Missions in 1702 and 1706, kidnapping around 1,000 Floridian Native Americans and forcing them into plantation slavery in the Carolinas. This move was supported by the British.

As Creek clans began to separate and form the Seminoles, relations with the British soured. The Seminoles were friendly enough with the Spanish, with whom they attempted peace talks, but the American invasions of Spanish Florida and the tension between armed white settlers and the new U.S. Government became too much.

Settlers who were moving south wanted Native American land. Many wealthy landowners wanted their former slaves back, some of whom had run to the sanctuary of Florida. Meanwhile, the new Seminole Tribe was prospering, and their numbers were increasing. They had made lots of money from trading with the British, and their economic success, combined with new crops, made Florida desirable again for the United States.

Relations with the Native Americans had never been particularly good for the new United States, but as the country began to grow and expand into the territory, they began pushing out those who had lived in the area for thousands of years. This was called Manifest Destiny — the belief that the U.S. was ordained by God to expand its territory throughout the American continents. Manifest Destiny wound up destroying millions of native lives and ended many ancient cultures throughout the continental United States, and the new territory of Florida was no exception.

As the Seminole nation grew in size and strength, they became more and more dangerous to the United States. They had already made themselves enemies to the United States; Seminoles and the runaway slaves who joined them were on amiable terms and had traded weapons with them and offered support during the War of 1812 against America. Preemptively, the United States Army invaded Florida and attacked the Seminoles, starting the first of three Seminole Wars.

The actual dates of the First Seminole War is unknown. The U.S. Army Infantry records show that the war lasted from 1814 to 1819; other sources date the war from 1816-1818. Still, some say it only lasted a year. However long the war actually lasted, it kicked off a series of conflicts and massacres that would plague Florida for many years.[24]

The Tragedy of Negro Fort

As the United States grew, they began to establish military bases around the borders of their territories. Fort Scott was established in the southwestern part of Georgia only a few miles from the Spanish border of Florida. The U.S. administration decided to send supplies through Spanish territory to the other side via the Apalachicola River. The Spanish protested but ultimately did nothing.

---

24. Gannon, 1996

The biggest problem for the United States was a small community of escaped slaves, Seminoles, and their descendants. They lived together at the so-called "Negro Fort," which sat 60 miles south of Fort Scott. It overlooked the river, and was occupied by 334 people who had stockpiled military supplies and weapons after the War of 1812.

A replica of the Negro Fort.

In 1816, Andrew Jackson led his troops into Florida, intent on destroying the fort. The United States wanted the fort eliminated to allow easy access to the Apalachicola River, but the government had other qualms with the fort. The cohabitation within the fort seemed to flout the principles of slavery and defied southern custom in the area. The U.S. wanted it eliminated to set an example of proper practice.

The men of Negro Fort refused to surrender and resubmit themselves to slavery. "Give me liberty, or give me death!" (a saying attributed to Patrick

Henry as a rallying cry for the Patriots during the Revolutionary War) was yelled out by men throughout the battle; ironic, considering the phrase's origin. The sides exchanged fire until a "hot shot" — or cannonball heated to a red glow — entered the fort's powder magazine where they kept their ammunition. The explosion was heard more than 100 miles away and killed all but 30 of the 300 occupants in the fort, including many women and children. This shot is still considered the single deadliest cannon shot in American history by historians. The few who survived were returned to slavery.[25]

A leader of the Seminole people, furious by the death of his people in the fort, issued a warning to the American general: any American forces crossing the Flint River would be attacked. The U.S. general sent 250 men to arrest the chief, and the resulting battle became what many consider the opening battle of the First Seminole War.[26]

Bloody Bloody Andrew Jackson

One of the most important American individuals in the Seminole Wars was Andrew Jackson, a man who would eventually become the seventh president of the United States.

Andrew Jackson was an icon in his time. He had the classic American Hero story — he grew up from rags to riches and was considered a true patriot by many Americans, who called him the "People's President." He had been orphaned at age 14 during the Revolutionary War and despised the British.

Jackson had risen to fame as a military figure and a national war hero after defeating the British in the Battle of New Orleans during the War of 1812. He destroyed the Second Bank of the United States and created the

---

25. Explore Southern History, 2017
26. Gannon, 2017

Democratic Party. Jackson was a firm believer in states' rights, and was responsible for the forced migration of thousands of Native American tribes.

Andrew Jackson, the seventh president of the United States.

Known as "Old Hickory" by his troops, Jackson was easily angered and often got into fights. Biographers noted that his opponents were terrified of Jackson's temper:

> "Observers likened him to a volcano, and only the most intrepid or recklessly curious cared to see it erupt . . . His close associates all had stories of his blood-curdling oaths, his summoning of the Almighty to loose His wrath upon some miscreant, typically followed by his own vow to hang the villain or blow him to perdition. Given his record — in

duels, brawls, mutiny trials, and summary hearings — listeners had to take his vows seriously . . ."[27]

During the War of 1812, Jackson led U.S. troops on a five-month campaign against the British-allied Creek Indians, who had massacred hundreds of settlers at Fort Mims in what is now present-day Alabama.

Andrew Jackson was the first U.S. President to have survived an assassination attempt. Richard Lawrence, a house painter, tried to shoot Jackson, but the gun misfired. Jackson then beat Lawrence with his cane (remember that temper?) until bystanders were able to subdue the would-be assassin.

On August 9, 1814, Andrew Jackson forced the Upper and Lower Towns of the Creek Nation to sign the Treaty of Fort Jackson. The Creeks were made to give 21,086,763 acres of land to the United States. He also forced the Creek to give up 1.9 million acres that was claimed as territory of the Cherokee Nation. This land is now present-day Alabama and southern Georgia. After this success, the U.S. military promoted Jackson to major general. Jackson was a native Southerner and had control of the army forces in the southern United States. When the government decided that the Seminoles had become a problem, he was called into action to defeat them.

Andrew Jackson Invades Florida

Jackson's direct orders from President Monroe were to "terminate the conflict" — and that was all the instruction he was given. To terminate the conflict, Jackson vowed to capture Florida from Spain once and for all. Before leaving for Florida, Jackson wrote to Monroe, "Let it be signified

---

27. Brands, 2005

to me through any channel . . . that the possession of the Floridas would be desirable to the United States, and in 60 days it will be accomplished."

President Monroe justified the First Seminole War to Congress by saying that the Seminoles had forced the United States' hand. He said that the United States was merely defending itself by attacking the Seminoles. Andrew Jackson said that his campaign was needed to "chastise a savage foe, combined with a lawless band of negro brigands" that were launching a "cruel and unprovoked war against the citizens of the United States."[28]

True to his word, Jackson invaded Florida on March 15, 1818. He captured Pensacola, believing that the Spanish were still supplying the Native Americans with guns and encouraging them to raid Alabama Territory. The Spanish defended the city, but left the area and took refuge in Fort San Carlos de Barrancas before eventually surrendering. The Spanish officials and soldiers were then forced to retreat to Havana, Cuba. The ship was later captured by corsairs, or pirates. Unfortunately, the ship was also carrying Pensacola's Spanish records, and the pirates threw all the documents overboard. Much of Pensacola's written history was lost forever to the sea that day.[29]

Jackson did not stop his advancement at Pensacola. As he marched onward, he crushed the Seminole and Spanish resistance in West Florida before marching to the Suwanee River. There, he captured two British citizens, Robert Chrystie Ambrister and Alexander Arbuthnot, suspecting them both of aiding the Native Americans and working against the United States. They were both tried at a judicial court for armed service members accused of offenses against military law. This practice is known as being court-martialed.

---

28. Gannon, 1996
29. Gannon, 1996

Both men were found guilty. Ambrister was shot by firing squad and Arbuthnot was hanged from his own ship, ironically named *The Last Chance*.[30]

The executions were a controversial move at the time and caused a diplomatic problem with the British. Two British subjects had been killed by American troops in Spanish territory. Although the British did not make a military move, the situation between the two nations became even tenser and was frightening to those who wished to resolve issues peacefully. The executions of Ambrister and Arbuthnot would tarnish Jackson's reputation forever.

Most citizens supported Jackson's actions in Florida, but some Americans worried that the "man on horseback" might become a military dictator. Jackson's actions in Florida upset President Monroe's cabinet and colleagues, who insisted that Jackson had violated the constitution because the United States had not officially declared war on either Spain or Britain.

Resolutions in Congress were introduced in 1818 to stop Jackson and remove him from Florida, but he was too popular with the American people, and the resolutions failed. He maintained his post, and continued conquering the territory. By 1818, St. Augustine was the only major town in Florida that remained under Spanish control. The Americans were swarming the Florida territory, and there was nothing the Spanish could do about it.

The Adams-Onís Treaty

The U.S. Army successfully invaded Florida under the command of Andrew Jackson. The Spanish held onto their territory for as long as they could but eventually caved to the pressure of the U.S. government.

---

30. Gannon, 1996

John Quincy Adams, the secretary of state, demanded that Spain control the rash actions of the inhabitants of East Florida or relinquish it to the United States. Meanwhile, Britain was still furious about the execution of two of its subjects who had never even entered United States territory. Americans were worried about the possibility of a new war with Britain.

Eventually, Spain caved and signed the Adams-Onís Treaty, and Britain dropped the case of Ambrister and Arbuthnot. This finally defined the boundary between the U.S. and the Spanish territories that had been unsure for so long. It settled the border argument between the two countries and was considered a triumph of American diplomacy. The treaty was 16 articles long and signed at Adams' State Department office in Washington, D.C. on February 22, 1819. Although it was approved by the U.S. Senate within days, Spanish officials delayed the approval until over a year later in October of 1820.

It took a year after that, in July 1821, for the American flag to replace the Spanish flag outside the Government House in Pensacola. Andrew Jackson himself supervised the ceremony.[31]

---

31. Gannon, 1996

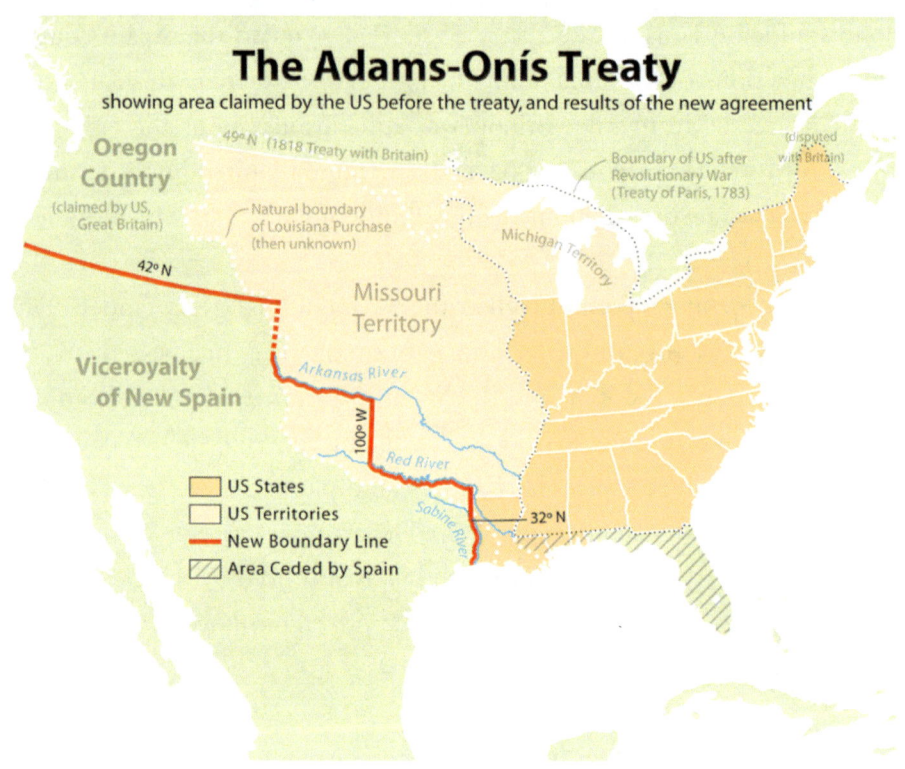

A map of the Adams-Onís Treaty.

Florida as a United States Territory

The most important elected official in the new Florida territory at the time was the territory's delegate to Congress. The first congressional delegate of Florida (and the first Hispanic to serve in Congress) was Joseph M. Hernandez, who was selected to serve in 1823. These delegates were elected by eligible votes, which, at the time, meant white males who were at least 21 and had lived in Florida for at least three months.

Because Florida was still not a state, delegates were not able to vote in Congress, but they could lobby, or influence, decisions about Florida in the U.S. government. Hernandez himself campaigned for naval projects and projects pertaining to the ocean, road construction, and bridges.

Florida's governors were never elected by the Floridian people. Instead, they were presidential appointees. Those who lived in Florida were more worried about acquiring land than political procedures in Washington, anyway.

At first, Andrew Jackson was established as the governor of Florida by President Monroe, but his time in office was brief. He was hot-tempered and once ordered that the Spanish governor, Jose Callava, be jailed for obstructing the delivery of lawsuit documents. His temper alarmed officials in Washington, who often voted against him. His nominees for important political offices were declined, and President Monroe chose the secretaries, judges, and attorneys instead.[32]

Jackson's position as governor scared the Seminoles. The United States government had begun removing Native Americans and sending them to reservations, and Jackson, known as "Sharp Knife," would do no less. Once he was elected president in 1828, there was no real hope for them, and the Indian Removal Law of 1830 only made things worse. This law let the president negotiate with southern Native American tribes for their removal in exchange for their lands. The removal act passed after a bitter debate in Congress.

Like many Americans, Jackson thought that the destruction of tribal nations would happen no matter what. He sincerely believed that his policy of removing Native Americans from their lands was the humanitarian option that would save the tribes from total annihilation through more forceful means. Native tribes had already nearly become extinct. Although some at the time viewed the Native American culture as a window into simpler times in the past, Jackson and his supporters disagreed. They argued that

---

32. Gannon, 1996

the Manifest Destiny was divinely ordained and inevitable, and Jackson himself said that "progress requires moving forward."[33]

Second Seminole War

By the 1820s, white settlers were driving the Floridian Native Americans toward war once again. Slavers preyed upon them and the free blacks living in Florida. In 1823, the government offered the Seminole a treaty known as the Treaty of Moultrie Creek. The agreement forced the Seminoles to give up their homeland to the U.S. and move even further south and required them to give runaway slaves back to their masters. In return, the Seminoles were promised 4 million acres of land south of modern-day Ocala. This land was called a reservation. The Seminoles' former home in Tallahassee became the capital of the Florida territory. The Seminoles became dependent on the government, and some even ran out of food.[34]

In the spring of 1832, the Seminoles living on the reservation were asked to a meeting with representatives from the government at Payne's Landing on the Oklawaha River. The treaty proposed by the United States called for the Seminoles to move west on the Creek reservation, becoming part of the Creek tribe. The seven Seminole chiefs appraised the new reservation and eventually signed a document on March 28, 1833 agreeing that the new land was acceptable.

When the chiefs returned to Florida, many said they had not actually signed the document. Some said that the Army forced them to sign it against their will. The chiefs claimed that they didn't have the authority to speak for all the tribes, and thus the agreement was invalid. Even some U.S. Army officers said that the chiefs had been bullied into signing the statement.

---

33. Brands, 2005
34. Florida Center for Instructional Technology, 2002

This did not matter to the U.S. government. The Senate ratified, or verified, the Treaty of Payne's Landing in April 1834. They wanted the Seminoles to move west of the Mississippi by 1835, even though the government claimed to have given the tribe three years to leave. With only one year remaining, time was running out.

The Seminole tribe did not feel bound by the Treaty of Payne's Landing and refused to move. An agreement was out of the question — they wanted to stay in their homelands. United States would have to force them to leave.

The man who brought the Seminoles together was named Osceloa. He was the son of an Englishman named William Powell and of a Creek woman called Polly Coppinger. White men called him Powell. He was not a chief, but he was the figurehead that inspired the Seminoles to keep their homeland away from the encroaching United States.[35]

Osceloa led the raid on several white armies. He destroyed plantations along the St. Johns River and fought ferociously against the United States Army. He and the Seminoles were determined to keep their homeland at all costs.

By 1835, there were around 800 to 1,400 Seminole warriors, with around 400 free black men as allies. They were fragmented into clans. Each clan had a chief, but there was no other government ruling over them.

Fearing violence, the U.S. banned the Seminoles from buying guns or ammunition. This was a bad move, and Osceloa in particular was furious. He said, "The white man shall not make me black. I will make the white man

---

35. Gannon, 1996

red with blood; and then blacken him in the sun and rain . . . and the buzzard live upon his flesh."[36]

Dade Massacre

On December 23, 1835, 110 U.S. troops left Fort Brooke (present day Tampa) to visit Fort King (present-day Ocala). The trip was dangerous. The Seminoles, furious at the U.S. Army, were following the troops closely. However, Major Francis L. Dade felt safe traveling along the King Highway military road. He believed there were no river crossings or thick woods to the south in which the native forces could hide and ambush him.

Dade was terribly wrong, though. The King Highway had plants like pines and palmettos, which were too thin to have concealed anyone standing, but did hide those crouching, waiting for the perfect time to attack.

Many Seminole warriors had secretly gathered at points along Dade's march. They watched the troops tirelessly at every turn, reporting their every move back to their chiefs. The Seminoles waited like this for five days, until December 28 when Dade and his troops were south of present-day Bushnell, Florida. A force of 180 Seminoles waited until 8 a.m. (or 10, depending on the account) when the troops were passing through a hammock, or strand of trees. The army saw pines, oaks, cabbage palms, and palmetto before someone shot and killed Major Dade. Only a few troops were able to grab their guns from beneath their hefty uniforms before they were set upon by the Native forces. The rest were killed in the surprise attack that did not end until around 4 p.m.

Seminole leader Halpatter Tustenuggee, who was known as Alligator by white men, had this to say about the attack:

---

36. Missall, 2004

"We had been preparing for this more than a year . . . Just as the day was breaking, we moved out of the swamp into the pine-barren. I counted, by direction of Jumper, 180 warriors. Upon approaching the road, each man chose his position on the west side . . . About nine o'clock in the morning the command approached . . . So soon as all the soldiers were opposite . . . Jumper gave the whoop, Micanopy fired the first rifle, the signal agreed upon, when every Indian arose and fired, which laid upon the ground, dead, more than half the white men. The cannon was discharged several times, but the men who loaded it were shot down as soon as the smoke cleared away . . . As we were returning to the swamp supposing all were dead, an Indian came up and said the white men were building a fort of logs. Jumper and myself, with 10 warriors, returned. As we approached, we saw six men behind two logs placed one above another, with the cannon a short distance off . . . We soon came near, as the balls went over us. They had guns, but no powder, we looked in the boxes afterwards and found they were empty."

Only three U.S. soldiers survived the attack. One man, Private Edward Decourcey, was covered by dead bodies and escaped detection. Ransom Clark had five wounds and bleeding cuts all over his body, but also managed to live. [37]

The next day, a Seminole warrior saw the pair and chased them on horseback. Decourcey was killed, but Clarke made it back to safety, collapsing within a mile of Fort Brooke, only making it back after being helped by a friendly Native American woman. Clarke provided the only story from the

---

37. Clarke, 1839

Army's side of what had occurred. A third survivor, Private Joseph Sprague, continued serving in the U.S. Army after returning to Fort Brooke. However, he could not write or read, and, as a result, never left his own account of the battle.

After the battle, the Seminoles burned plantations and killed settlers all across Florida. By 1836, only one house in Miami-Dade and Broward counties still stood. The battle had not only killed Floridians, but also new immigrants and residents from other states. The news of Dade Massacre was reported in the Daily National Intelligencer in Washington, D.C. in the Wednesday, January 27, 1836 edition:

> "Major Dade, with seven officers and 110 men, started the day before we arrived, for Fort King. We were all prepared to overtake them the next day . . . when an intervention of circumstances deferred it for one day — and in the course of that day, three soldiers, horribly mangled, came into camp, and brought the melancholy tidings that Major Dade, and every officer and man, except themselves, were murdered and terribly mangled."

The massacre totally dominated the newspapers, and President Andrew Jackson called for new volunteers to the U.S. Army from Florida, Georgia, and South Carolina. The Second Seminole War had begun, and would be the longest of the Seminole Wars, lasting from 1835 to 1842.

A painting of the Dade Massacre.

You can visit the Dade Battlefield Historic National Park today. There are often reenactments of the historic battle!

The Second War Rages On

The Second Seminole War left confusion and destruction everywhere in its path. Slave catchers were kidnapping black people living with the Seminoles and forcing them into servitude. The Seminoles had no written record of ownership, so it was easy for the catchers to take free men and women and send them back to slave states. Other whites wanted the Seminoles arrested for alleged crimes or debts.[38]

The United States Army in Florida only had one commander position, but seven men served in the role during the Second Seminole War. Tensions between generals led to fighting within the American forces. In one in-

---

38. Missall, 2004

stance, two generals vilified each other so much that a court of inquiry, or questioning, needed to be called to settle a dispute.

By December 1837, Colonel Zachary Taylor, who later became the 12th president of the United States, went to Lake Okeechobee to round up Seminole Indians resisting removal from the land. He and his troops were ambushed by around 400 Seminoles under chiefs Alligator, Billy Bowlegs, and Abiaca.

The Seminoles had surveyed the site, even cutting the grass to prepare a field of fire. They carefully selected their targets, and many of the dead and wounded were officers. In the end, of the two and a half hour battle, 26 U.S. soldiers were killed and 112 were wounded. On the Seminole side, only 11 were killed and 14 wounded, but they had scattered into the forest.

Taylor was forced to retreat, but the event gained the public's attention, and he became a brigadier general. He was one of the only American commanders to receive positive publicity for the Second Seminole War.[39]

Meanwhile, U.S. forces finally captured Osceola.[40] They misled him by waving a white flag symbolizing truce and capturing him as he arrived. He was imprisoned in the Spanish fortress Castillo de San Marcos at St. Augustine, which was also known as Fort Marion. Osceola died in prison in 1838.

Support for the Second Seminole War was ending in Washington, D.C. and throughout the rest of the United States by 1839. The Army had grown because of the need for troops in Florida. Many thought the Seminoles should stay in Florida, and the cost to move them to a reservation was

39. U-S History, n.d.
40. USWars, 2012

enormous. Congress and President Martin Van Buren tried to negotiate with the Seminoles, and eventually both sides agreed — they would stop fighting and resettle at a reservation in southern Florida.[41]

The peace did not last long, though. After a trading post was attacked in July 1839 by a raiding band of Native Americans, the war was on again. Some thought that certain civilians wanted to deliberately prolong the war to continue being paid by the government. Raids from both sides were common, and civilians were often caught in the crossfire.[42]

There were battles nearly everywhere the white settlers lived. The Seminoles would attack white settlers and then disappear into the forests, ambushing them when they least expected it. In turn, when Seminoles and free blacks were captured, they were often shipped west or forced into slavery.

Although the Seminoles knew the area and fought ferociously, the American army forced them further and further south into the wilderness of the Everglades. The Seminoles were determined to stay in Florida.

Outcomes of the War

When Colonel Worth became the commander of the United States Army in Florida, he divided his forces. Some removed Seminoles from Northern Florida, while others marched through the swamps of South Florida. He also reduced the number of civilians and militiamen employed by the United States.

Worth's campaign finally put an end to the Second Seminole War. By 1842, only 300 Native Americans remained in Florida. 112 of them were warriors; the rest were women and children. They were miserable and hungry

---

41. Missall, 2004
42. Mahon, 1967

and tired of fighting. The War Department (as it was then known) eventually allowed them to live in a 6,700 square-mile southern reservation.[43]

The Second Seminole War officially ended. Thousands of people from both sides died, and it cost more than $30 million. It was also an uneasy peace, which would eventually break and lead to the Third Seminole War in 1855.

At the end of the war, Congress passed the Armed Occupation Act (AOA) of 1842. This encouraged whites to move to Florida and forced any remaining Seminoles to leave the area. The act said that any white man or head of the family that was capable of armed defense could take 160 acres of land south of Gainesville and north of the Peace River. Around 1,200 people received 200,000 acres of land, and 6,000 people moved to Florida as a direct result of the act.

Hillsborough County began to grow. There were only 92 people living in Hillsborough in 1840, but as the AOA gained popularity, more and more families began to move there. Southern Aristocratic families like the Braden, Gamle, and Craig found success as they moved their plantations along the Manatee River, discovering a better growing season for sugarcane. By 1860, more than 900 people lived along the prosperous Manatee plantations. It was a new American frontier — a hot, humid, and Floridian frontier.[44]

---

43. Gannon, 1996
44. Gannon, 1996

Chapter 4
Florida Becomes a State

"The dreamers line the state road
Just to watch the runway show
Slouched behind their steering wheels
They just watch the big jets go
Streakin' through the morning haze
Focal point of a distant gaze
Lookin' for better days

Pale invaders and tanned crusaders
Are worshipping the sun
On the corner of "walk" and "don't walk"
Somewhere on U.S. 1
I'm back to livin' Floridays
Blue skies and ultra-violet rays
Lookin' for better days"
— Jimmy Buffett, Floridays

Under the United States, the economy of Florida began to flourish. The newspaper Florida Republican reported that Jacksonville had the largest lumber market in the South. Mills cut yellow pine and shipped Florida timber internationally. Railroads began their own timberlands, encouraging new farmers to grow trees. New homesteads were cleared for settlement.

As the business began to thrive and population swelled, government influence grew too. The government was dominated by a group of men known as the "Nucleus." They were appointed by Presidents Monroe and Jackson, and most were aristocrats who had gained control of the Florida Land Office. They were slave owners, cotton planters, and members of the Whig Political Party. Their terrible bank policy became one of the most controversial political issues in Florida, eventually leading to the territory become a state in 1845.

Bank Wars Begin

Between 1831 and 1835, the Legislative Council of Florida approved bank charters (or the ability to become a bank) for groups in Pensacola, Tallahassee, and St. Augustine. Everyone who received those bank loans were part of the ruling elite in Florida and were able to easily get loans from members of the government, many of whom were their friends and relatives. As the banks grew, those who owned them began inflating the value of mortgages on land, letting planters receive bigger loans to purchase more land and more slaves. Sales were made possible by the "good faith" promise of the Legislative Council — this meant that they would pay the loans back, no matter what.

However, sometimes nature has other ideas. In the winter of 1835, a bitter frost destroyed the citrus industry in East Florida. The Second Seminole War had already disrupted the territory, and when the Panic of 1837 hit, leading to bank failures throughout the nation, the legislative council passed laws to tax Florida residents to pay interest on the "good faith" bonds from years past. Florida residents were outraged, viewing the Nucleus politicians as corrupt, failing to serve the people whom they represented. Politicians who were outside the inner circle saw their chance to replace the corrupt politicians, and began campaigning against the Nucleus, forming groups like the Jacksonian Democratic Party to get rid of the aristocrats in power.

An 1836 political cartoon of the Bank War.

Florida's Bank War paved the way for the territory to become a state. If Florida became a state, the ruling Nucleus class would theoretically have less power. Some pointed to the millions of acres of land in the territory controlled by Congress that could be given to Florida and used by state officials. They claimed that the economy and population would grow if Florida became a state.

In 1838, a poll showed that a majority of voters wanted Florida to become a state, and a convention was held at St. Joseph, a new port near Apalachicola, to elect new delegates. Candidates pledged to anti-banking positions and vowed never to support aristocrats who had profited from the banks and hurt the working class. Unsurprisingly, the anti-bank delegates won most of the seats. Some were future governors, others were future U.S. senators like David Levy Yulee. Yulee would go on to be the first Jewish person to serve in the U.S. Senate, and was the founder and president of the Florida Railroad.

The delegates debated until January 11, 1839, when a constitution for Florida was finally approved. It specifically restricted the banking policies that had so hurt Florida's economy.[45]

A Push for Statehood

Congressional delegate Yulee was incredibly influential to Florida becoming a member of the Union. He wrote letters, gave speeches, and delivered pamphlets promoting statehood. Yulee claimed that if Florida became a state, the U.S. Congress would make federal lands in the territory available to support the railroads and other projects. This would make Florida important to the rest of the United States, and more people would move south.

Yulee traveled to Washington, D.C., trying to convince southern congressmen to vote Florida into the Union. He reminded them that if Florida became a state, it would have to allow slavery in order for its economy to survive. Iowa was about to become a free state and outlaw slavery, so if Florida became a state at the same time, it would even out the number of free states and slave states — an all-important necessity for slave-states in Washington.[46]

His reminder worked. In January 1845, the House of Representatives approved a bill that made both Florida and Iowa states. The bill was signed

---

45. Gannon, 1996
46. Gannon, 1996

by President John Tyler on March 3, 1845. Florida was now the 27th state, following Iowa.

 What's the flattest state in the whole United States? Nope, not Kansas. According to National Geographic, it's actually Florida![47]

Third Seminole War

In August 1842, Billy Bowlegs became the principal chief over 300-400 Native Americans who remained in Florida; only 20 Seminole warriors refused to recognize him as their chief. He became a trusted leader who attempted to keep the peace between his people and the U.S. government.

But the peace would not last. Seven years after the Seminoles and the United States signed their peace treaty, five young warriors destroyed settlements and killed Americans outside of the reservation. Bowlegs attempted to capture the criminals to help bring them to justice. He found three and killed one other, but the fifth criminal escaped.

While Bowlegs had cooperated with the government and even aided in their attempts to punish the criminals, Floridians didn't care. They saw the whole group as troublemakers and wanted the Seminoles out of the area altogether. One St. Augustine newspaper from 1852 recommended that all natives be outlawed and a $1,000 bounty be offered for every Seminole male caught alive or dead, and $500 for women and children. Senator Stephen Mallory proclaimed that the Seminoles had to leave or be killed.

---

47. Howard, 2014

For many years, the United States had tried to remove the Native Americans without war. They tried to persuade Native Americans to venture west and leave the area occupied by American whites. In 1850, Major General David Twiggs even offered Native Americans $10,000 per person if they left Florida peacefully. Understandably, the Seminoles didn't take the bait. Money wasn't the issue. They didn't want to be forced out by soldiers with guns or by passive-aggressive bribes. This was their home. They would stay and fight for their territory and their right to stay free.

Jefferson Davis, the secretary of war for the U.S. government (who would later become the President of the Confederacy during the Civil War), listened to the white Floridians. He stopped all trade to the reservation and sent the Army to patrol abandoned roads. Military boats even began to appear in the swamps where some Seminoles lived. Davis wanted the message made clear to the Seminoles: leave your home or face the wrath of the United States.

On December 18, 1855, 30 native warriors opened fire on Lt. George Hartstuff's military detachment of 10 men. The Seminoles wounded four and killed four. This conflict officially pushed the Seminoles and the United States into the third and final Seminole War.

The odds were against the Native Americans from the beginning. The United States had around 1,500 soldiers at their disposal, while the Seminoles had only around 100 warriors. This meant that there were around 14 American soldiers for each Seminole. However, while the U.S. had far greater numbers than the Seminoles, they had a hard time organizing their army, and there was often miscommunication between the federal and state commanders.

On the other hand, the Seminoles had no real planned strategy, but they attacked isolated camps and residencies. For six months, they attacked the United States. By the end, they made 15 raids and killed 28 people.

The governor of Florida, James Broome, ordered militia companies into service, insisting that citizen soldiers were the only way to defeat the Seminoles. He called for 10 companies in 1857, but some were not accepted by the War Department and were never paid for their service.

In September 1856, Brigadier General William S. Harney returned to command the federal troops in Florida. He remembered the lessons he had learned in the Second Seminole War and created a line of forts across Florida. Patrols moved deeper into Seminole territory, intending to make the Seminoles retreat into the Big Cypress Swamp and the Everglades. Harney guessed that the Seminoles would not be able to survive there during the wet season and hoped to catch them as they left the flooded wetlands looking for dry land. However, this tactic showed few results, and Harney and his men were transferred to Kansas after only a year in Florida.[48]

Another colonel, Gustavus Loomis, became the commander in Florida. Loomis organized his men into boat companies, giving them metal "alligator boats." The boats were 30 feet (9.1 meters) long, pointed at both ends, and could carry 16 people into the swamps. Using the alligator boats, the United States army captured many Seminole women and children.[49]

By 1858, federal troops had captured Seminoles and destroyed crops and towns, and Billy Bowlegs finally accepted money to move his tribe west out of Florida. He was paid $6,500 for himself, $1,000 for four sub-chiefs, $500 for other warriors, and $100 for women and children. 164 Seminoles

---

48. Covington, 1993
49. Covington, 135-43

left for New Orleans on May 4, 1858, receiving a total of $44,600. Some Seminoles, like the ancient Sam Jones, remained secluded on an island in the Everglades. He died there, supposedly at the amazing age of 111.

The Third Seminole War had almost extinguished Native American culture in Florida, but around 200 native peoples still remained; they were able to preserve some of their culture. They mostly withdrew from the influence of cultures beyond their own and lived in the lower portion of Florida in small camps along the Everglades.

These small groups slowly grew and rebuilt new cultures and traditions from their old heritage. Like the early Seminoles, the natives lived in thatched huts. They traveled between islands via dugout canoes, and traded with other Seminole groups for cloth, corn, pots, rifles, and ammunition. The Green Corn Dance was still practiced, and each group carried a medicine bundle, a gathering of sacred objects.[50]

---

50. Gannon, 1996

Chapter 5
The Civil War in Florida

Mine eyes have seen the glory of the coming of the Lord;
He is trampling out the vintage where the grapes of wrath
  are stored;
He hath loosed the fateful lightning of His terrible swift
  sword;
His truth is marching on.
Glory! Glory! Hallelujah!
Glory! Glory! Hallelujah!
Glory! Glory! Hallelujah!
His truth is marching on.
— Lee Greenwood, Battle Hymn of the Republic

Following the Seminole War, another dramatic conflict began to influence the peninsula. This war ripped families apart, razed whole portions of the South, and changed the political, social, and economic landscape of America forever. It was the "War Between the States" — the American Civil War.

Although Florida had managed to escape the Revolutionary War unscathed, residents could not ignore the consequences of the Civil War. Their entire economy depended on slave labor, and as the topic of slavery began to be more hotly debated in Washington, D.C., Floridians — and the influential plantation owners — became nervous.

Like most Southern states, Democrats were in charge in Florida. At that time, the Democratic party became focused on states' rights and demanded the right to leave the Union (another term for the U.S.) almost immediately after they became a state in 1845. They were demanding "Southern Rights" — or the right to own slaves and to move slaves into western territories of the United States. They called it "defense of property," but really, it was about owning free labor.

Slave labor was vital to the Floridian economy. Enslaved blacks had always worked the land in Florida while the Spanish and the British were in control, so why should it be any different under the Americans? The population of slaves grew as more people — and more plantation owners — moved into the territory. In 1860, 50 percent of the total population of Jefferson County consisted of enslaved black people. Free blacks were rarely seen in the state, especially in the middle of Florida, although some still lived in areas like St. Augustine.

When the Spanish were in control, they had a three-caste system: white owners, free blacks, and black slaves. However, after the United States took control, there were only slaves and white owners. Many blamed the presence of free blacks for slave uprisings, so harsh punishments and unfair laws were passed against free blacks, causing many to relocate to other places such as Mexico or Haiti. A St. Augustine newspaper labeled free blacks as "useless" and "hopeless, degraded, wretched, and forbidden outcasts," in 1851, reacting to the hysteria and white supremacy that escalated and eventually began the Civil War.

By 1861, there were 61,000 slaves in Florida. They were vital to the state's cotton production — around 85 percent of cotton in Florida was produced through their labor. They also worked in fisheries and salt worksand transported supplies for the Confederate army. White Floridians lived in fear that the Union would inspire slaves to run away, revolt, or kill their masters.

In 1860, the Democrats in Florida joined with other Democrats in southern states to block candidate Stephen Douglas from becoming the Democratic nominee for president. They believed that he jeopardized their right to bring slaves into western territories, and when Northern Democrats insisted on Douglas, the Southerners broke from them and backed another candidate, John C. Breckenridge of Kentucky. Meanwhile, the Republicans chose Abraham Lincoln.

On November 7, 1860, Election Day, Democrats were horribly disappointed. Douglas had received only 367 votes, while a candidate from the Constitutional Union Party had polled 5,437 votes. Breckenridge had received 8,543 votes and was supported by 18 of the state's 24 newspapers. Abraham Lincoln was not even on the ballot in Florida, but he won the presidency anyway, becoming the nation's 16th president.

White Southerners and Floridians were furious by Lincoln's victory. After his election, there were even more mob rallies and calls for Florida and other states to secede and leave the Union. A story in the *Tallahassee Floridian and Journal* even read, "Lincoln is elected. There is a beginning of the end. Sectionalism has triumphed. What is to be done? We say resist."

Finally, tensions reached a breaking point, and South Carolina seceded from the Union on December 20th, 1860. They would not recognize the United States as their government and would make their own laws instead.

Florida was not far behind. On January 10, delegates in Florida voted 62 to seven to leave the Union. By February 4, representatives were sent to

Montgomery, Alabama to form the government of the Confederate States of America. Florida changed their flag, wrote another constitution, and held new elections. The confederate states eventually included South Carolina, North Carolina, Virginia, Georgia, Alabama, Mississippi, Louisiana, Tennessee, Texas, and Arkansas. Jefferson Davis, a Mississippian, became President of the Confederacy, and Montgomery, Alabama was chosen as the capital (although it was soon moved to Richmond, Virginia).[51]

The War Begins

Tensions were running high across the United States, and war seemed inevitable. It was only a matter of time before violence broke out; skirmishes between secessionists and Union troops had already begun. One of these skirmishes took place in Pensacola and was nearly the first battle of the Civil War.

January 1861 began with a fight between Union Lieutenant Adam J. Slemmer and the new Confederacy. Slemmer could not hold his troops around Pensacola and instead took his men to Fort Pickens, located at the entrance to Pensacola Bay. The fort, located on Santa Rosa Island, blocked the largest harbor used by the Confederacy. The Confederacy hoped to take it away from Slemmer by force, and the Lincoln administration scrambled to create a strategy for the Union troops. But tempers were high, and before the fight began in Pensacola Bay, Fort Sumter was attacked by South Carolinians, starting the bloodiest war in American history.

---

51. Gannon, 1996

An aerial view of Fort Sumter.

After Fort Sumter, President Lincoln asked for 75,000 willing men to end the southern rebellion. In response, white male Floridians rushed to join the Confederacy and fight for their "Southern Rights." Florida had the smallest population of all the seceded southern states, and nearly half of that was made up of slaves. As a result, Florida sent just 15,000 men to the Confederate Army. Many of these men left Florida altogether to join the growing rebel armies, never to return to their homes.

Relatively few battles were actually fought in Florida because it was so far from Virginia and other, more resource-rich, states, but because it provided much of the food supply to the South and had long coastlines that were hard for the Union to properly patrol, the state was still very important to the war effort. The farmland in central Florida had more cows than people, and the Confederacy came to rely on beef production for food. Florida also produced a lot of salt, which was essential to preserving meat and tanning leather for the army. Before the Civil War, production of salt had come mainly from salt mines in the Upper South and from the Caribbean islands, but by the spring of 1862, the South faced a salt famine. So, instead of delving further into the mines, they turned to Florida with its long coastline and abundant source of oceanic salt-water.

Saltworks of all sizes sprang up along Florida coasts, from large production factories to single-home families using sugar kettles to boil ocean water for the leftover salt. Slaves often worked at the saltworks, but they were also joined by white men who avoided the draft by supplying the army with this much-needed commodity.

The Union soon learned about the South's salt production and began to attack it at its sources. Landing parties of Union soldiers attempted to destroy salt plants, but most saltworks were prepared for invasion and often resumed production shortly after destruction. In any case, the Union Army did not consider Florida too significant to the Confederacy's strategy, so the state was left relatively alone and was able to continue making salt for the Confederacy until the end of the war.

The Union, recognizing the significance of Florida's demographics, began heavily recruiting black troops from Florida — particularly those from the northeastern part of the state. Many of the black recruits established all-black regiments that would become historically famous like the 54th Massachusetts Colored Infantry, whose troops would later become heroes at the Battle of Olustee in Florida.[52]

Thinking about moving to Florida? You're not alone. More than 1,000 people move there every day![53]

---

52. Gannon, 1996
53. State of Florida, n.d.

Unsurprisingly, the Confederate army did not appreciate the Union's recruitment of their black residents, and the South's dismay did not go unnoticed up north. The commanding general of the Union wrote to Washington, D.C., "It is my belief that scarcely an incident in this war has caused greater panic throughout the whole Southern coast than this raid of colored troops in Florida."[54]

War Toils On . . .

By 1863, the Civil War was beginning to take its toll on the country. While the men were at war, women were left at home. While wealthy women could rely on their savings, relatives, and their slaves to maintain their way of life, others who were not so fortunate began demanding aid from the government. Slaves often ran away to freedom with the invading Yankees, as the Union troops were known by the Southerners. Florida was hardly industrialized but was rather a state full of small family farms, so stores quickly ran out of supplies. To make matters worse for the South, the Union blockade made prices on common items like coffee skyrocket. Pork soared to an unthinkable $50 a barrel, or $939.02 by today's standards. Starvation was a very real danger.

Strict policies from the Confederate government, like the unpopular 1862 Conscription Act, which made all white males between the ages of 18 and 35 eligible to be drafted into military service, rubbed Floridian residents the wrong way. Although many supported "the cause" initially, these acts from the government turned many against the Confederacy. Many sections of the state were overrun by armed bands of Union soldiers, gangs of draft evaders, and army deserters. These groups often clashed violently, terrorizing the communities caught in the midst. By now, it was truly a Civil War — a war between citizens of the same country.

---

54. Saxton, 1863

The Northern government, much like the United States a century before, schemed to reclaim the peninsula as their own. They sent Yankees south to look for recruits and eventually managed to find enough volunteers in the southern state for two regiments in the Union Army.

Union soldiers stationed in Florida often had a very different experience than those who were based in other southern states. They invaded many Florida cities but were met with little Confederate resistance, as most Floridian men were off fighting elsewhere. Most of the attacks in Florida by the Union Army were more like "expeditions" or raids to find cattle or other supplies that would make their life more comfortable rather than actual battles. If they found slaves, they freed them; if there was cotton, the soldiers would take it; if there was food or shelter, they helped themselves. Men from the northern states were pleasantly surprised to be met with citrus and palm trees during a bloody war, and the warm weather was idealistic compared to the bitter temperatures of a New England winter. Some men even swore never to return to their hometowns.

What fighting and battles there were in Florida were relatively tame and low-casualty compared to sites like the Battle of Gettysburg. In fact, there was only one significant battle in Florida during the whole of the war: the clash in Olustee.

The Battle of Olustee and the Fighting 54th

It was 1864, and the Union Army was eyeing Florida. Generals thought that capturing the state would hold numerous advantages for the North. Florida was supplying livestock to the Confederate Army, so cutting off this food supply would make the already-starving rebel troops even hungrier and weaker. President Lincoln was also trying to get Florida back into the Union so he could win the three more electoral votes in the 1864 presidential election.

The Union Army moved from Jacksonville toward Lake City, the largest city between Jacksonville and the panhandle. However, they never made it there.

Confederate troops from Florida intercepted the Union soldiers, stopping the advance. Each side had about 5,000 troops, but the Confederates sent in their troops all at once, while the North sent in their men one unit at a time, each unit made up of around 1,000 men.

The 54th was ordered forward as the Union troops retreated. They held the line as the northern troops dropped their guns in a panic, saving the Union army from further destruction. As the Union army ran out of ammunition, they fell back. 86 of the 500 men in the Fighting 54th were killed, but they had staved off the advancing Union army. They began the weary journey back to Jacksonville — a nearly 120-mile march. The Fighting 54th became famous for their courage and stopped the North's effort to retake Florida. The Union army would never gain complete control of the state until the end of the war.

A painting of the Battle of Olustee.

In the South, the battle was a morale-booster — a sign that the Confederacy was alive and well. One Georgia newspaper referred to Union forces as having walked "40 miles over the most barren land of the South, frightening the salamanders and the gophers, and getting a terrible thrashing."[55]

The Fighting 54th eventually found their way into America's history books and even onto the big screen. The movie "Glory" depicts a dramatized version of the battle.

End of the War

Florida may have remained under Confederate control, but the South was rapidly losing power in the war. They were wanting to hold out at least until the presidential election in 1864, hoping that northerners would vote Lincoln out of office and his successor might negotiate a peace deal. However, this was not the case. Lincoln was reelected to a second term, and on January 31, 1865, the 13th Amendment was enacted, abolishing slavery in the United States. Only three months later, on April 9, 1865, the Civil War officially ended in a victory for the federal government.

It took a few days for the news to reach Florida, and the official surrender of the Confederacy to the Union came on April 26. The war was finally over. The state of Florida was now once more a member of the Union.[56] The boys who had gone off to fight could finally return home in peace. However, of the 5,500 soldiers who left Florida to fight, 1,500 of them did not come home.[57]

1865 marked the end of the Civil War and a final push for northern control in Florida. Union soldiers rowed ashore in Florida to capture Tallahas-

55. Wynne, 2001
56. Dunn, 2016
57. Clark, 2014

see, but stubborn residents there built trenches to defend themselves that can still be seen today.

Confederate General Robert E. Lee surrendered to a Union general, Ulysses S. Grant in Virginia in the spring of 1865. Floridians, tired of fighting, accepted the defeat and the end of the war — for the most part. Governor John Milton left Tallahassee to return to his plantation, "Sylvania," in Marianna, Florida, and wrote a final letter to the state legislature.

"'Yankees' have developed a character so odious that death would be preferable to reunion with them," he wrote in his message. The governor made good on his promise. On April 1, 1865, he committed suicide at Sylvania, preferring a gunshot to the head rather than watching the despised Yankees take over the state. The president of the Florida Senate, Abraham K. Allison, was sworn in as governor of Florida that same day.[58]

The Floridians who had fought in the Confederate army began making their way home. Union troops raised the American flag over Tallahassee, Florida's capital city, proclaiming victory on May 20. The Civil War was finally over.

The state emerged from the other side in much better condition than its Confederate neighbors, but it still suffered in the wake of devastation. A crippled economy and a population of newly-freed slaves made many residents nervous. Money and credit from the Confederacy was now worthless, and the means of production that had been the norm for the state for so long ended once the slaves were freed. There were no markets and hardly any forms of transportation. Union soldiers and ex-Confederates had to learn how to live together. The end of the Civil War would usher in a new time for the United States — and the sunny state of Florida.

58.

Chapter 6

Reconstruction

"One reads the truer deeper facts of Reconstruction with a great despair. It is at once so simple and human, and yet so futile. There is no villain, no idiot, no saint. There are just men; men who crave ease and power, men who know want and hunger, men who have crawled. They all dream and strive with ecstasy of fear and strain of effort, balked of hope and hate. Yet the rich world is wide enough for all, wants all, needs all. So slight a gesture, a word, might set the strife in order, not with full content, but with growing dawn of fulfillment. Instead roars the crash of hell . . ."
— W.E.B. Du Bois, Black Reconstruction in America 1860-1880

The Florida government was in shambles after the Civil War. Governor Milton had died by suicide, and the Union General Edward McCook halted efforts to reorganize a new government that could raise a new crop of Confederate politicians. President Lincoln, assassinated by John Wilkes Booth on April 14, was the only person who planned to bring the seceded states back into the Union and help reconstruct them properly.

This period of time immediately after the Civil War is called Reconstruction. It was a time of uncertainty for the southern people. In the chaos, military officials took over.

Federal troops were still in Florida during the 1876 presidential election, and they controlled almost everything. Thanks to the federal government and new African-American voters, Republican Rutherford B. Hayes became the president of the United States.

Meanwhile, the anti-Confederate feeling in Washington, D.C. was declining. Many of the politicians who had been in charge during the Civil War had either died or retired, and the anger boiling underneath the surface for many men became just a childhood memory. Most southern states had regained control and federal troops had left. Only South Carolina, Louisiana, and Florida remained under the federal government control.

Although a Republican had become president, largely thanks to Floridians, the Democrats came back into power state-wide. George Drew, a Democrat who was friends with the old Confederates, became governor of Florida. Although he won by a slim margin, he signified the start of a new era: nearly a century of total Democratic control over the Sunshine state.

With the southern Democrats back in power, they agreed to go along with the Republicans in Washington and the new president, Rutherford B. Hayes, in exchange for the end of the Reconstruction period. Federal troops posted down south disappeared, leaving Floridians to their own devices. Unfortunately, this meant that the rights former slaves had been steadily gaining since the end of the war all but disappeared as well.

Rutherford B. Hayes, the 19th president of the United States

One of the biggest issues after the Civil War was farming, an important part of Florida's economy. The plantation owners now found themselves without workers because they had formerly relied on the free labor of slaves. Worse, the freed slaves, or freedmen, did not have jobs or own land with which they could survive on their own. Most had no skills and no schooling, without which they could not find work, so they returned back to the plantations they knew so well. However, because the plantation owners had no money after the war, they could not afford to pay the freedmen.

This led to sharecropping. Freed slaves could "rent" a piece of property on the plantation, as long as they gave the owner of the plantation a share of their harvest, or crop.

The plantation owners then provided housing, materials, and machinery needed for farming the land. Although it sounded like a better deal than slavery, sharecropping held far more advantage for plantation owners than the freed slaves.[59]

Gatorade was named for the University of Florida Gators — that's where the drink was first created.[60]

Racism in Florida

Slavery was declared extinct by the federal government in Washington D.C, but their proclamations were not always followed down south.

The newly elected governor, David Walker, seemed to believe that the Civil War was not over, and the Confederates were still in charge. An 1865 convention secured the Thirteenth Amendment, freeing the slaves, but Walker and many other governors in the former Confederate states passed new laws called Black Codes. There was even a special committee dedicated to the continuation of the "benign, but much abused and greatly misunderstood institution of slavery."[61]

Black Codes in Florida

Most white southerners did not want blacks to have the same rights as them, and Floridians were no exception. Their legislature passed Black Codes in 1866 to force former slaves to continue working for low wages. It was slavery by a different name.

59. Florida Center for Instructional Technology, 2002
60. Striepe, 2013
61. Clark, James, 2014

The Black Codes forced former slaves to continue working, and it made it almost impossible for them to gain social status. Vagrancy laws meant that men who were out of work or not working a "valuable" job could be forced to work one year of hard labor. If convicted, their children were hired out as apprentices under a skilled employer.

This law referred to "any person of color" or someone who had at least one black great-grandparent. This racist law was supported by the legal system and those in power, and it took decades for Black Codes to be officially removed from the legislature.

Black Lawmakers

Attempts to stop freemen from gaining their rights did not always work. A few black men even managed to become politicians. One of these men was Jonathan Gibbs.

He was the first African American to hold statewide office in Florida. He was the secretary of state and the superintendent of public instruction. A carpenter by trade, he eventually became a minister and worked with Frederick Douglass in the abolitionist movement. He preached in Philadelphia during the war, but moved south to help with newly-freed slaves as the Civil War ended. In 1867, he moved to Jacksonville and started a private school.

During this time, Gibbs became interested in politics. His religion and political stance reflected the attitudes of many black officeholders. Charles H. Pearce, another prominent black politician, said, "A man in this state, cannot do his whole duty as a minister except he looks out for the political interests of his people,"[62] Gibbs thought no differently. He was even

---

62. Brown, 1946

involved in writing the 1868 Florida Constitution, although most of his contributions failed.

Jonathan Gibbs, the first African American to hold a statewide office position in Florida.

Gibbs became Florida's secretary of state in 1868 and became the superintendent of public instruction in 1873. He also became a colonel in the state militia and was elected to the Tallahassee City Council.

As secretary of state, he launched investigations into racist groups like the new Ku Klux Klan; as a superintendent, he began creating a public school system. However, the legislature had already separated white children and black children into two separate school systems, and he had limited financial resources.

In 1874, Gibbs died after suffering a heart attack. It was rumored that he was poisoned, but that has never been proven.

Tourists Begin Visiting Florida

As Reconstruction ended, Florida began to revitalize its economy. One of the main ways the state made money was through tourism.

At first, only rich people could afford to visit Florida on vacation. They loved the warm weather and sandy beaches, and some even loved the area so much that they stayed to farm or start another a business.

After visiting in 1883, Henry S. Flagler, an oil baron, decided to stay in Florida to become one of the most influential developers in the region. He used his vast wealth to build hotels and railroads. In 1890, the railways to Florida were finally completed, and people from as far away as New York could finally visit. They marveled at the palm trees and oceans, basked in the sun and luxury of new hotels, and even visited to cure illnesses in the humid weather.

The famous and wealthy like Thomas Edison, Henry Ford, and Harriet Beecher Stove owned winter homes and stayed for months. Once cars were invented, travel became even more convenient.

Although travel methods had become more affordable, lodging was still expensive. Some tourists brought along their own beds and food, and slept in their cars to avoid the high-priced hotels. Because the food they brought along was often stored in tin cans, these travelers became known as "tin-can tourists." [63]

---

63. Florida Center for Instructional Technology, 2002

Then came the planes. In the 1930s, airlines began booking flights to Florida. This made travel even easier and even more tourists visit the state. Airports were built in more and more major cities.

After World War II, Florida's economy was supported in large part by tourism. Initially, there wasn't much to do in Florida beyond admiring the unique natural beauty. Travelers came and admired the sandy beaches; the Everglades with its alligators, panthers and birds; and the coral reefs and fishing of the Florida Keys. They could hike, boat, fish, and swim throughout the state. But most visitors came for one reason above all — sunshine.

Everglade National Park

For thousands of years, water in south Florida stretched a span of almost 11,000 miles, creating ponds and marshes — an ecosystem that was unlike any other. However, to settlers and developers, the Everglades were potential farmlands and communities. They began to drain the Everglades from wetland to "civilized" country in the 1900s, severely damaging the ecosystem and the species it supported in the process.

In 1910, 49 people lived in Flamingo and Cape Sable, most of whom were sugar-cane farmers. Some residents made charcoal, which was then sent to Key West. Early settlers also depended on hunting small game and fishing for food. Plume feathers were a popular addition to ladies' hats at the time, so hunting the brightly colored birds of the Everglades was also a major source of income. Some birds killed for those hats are now extinct today because they were overhunted.

An aerial view of Everglade National Park.

Life in the Everglades could be awful at times. Leverett White Brownell described the village in 1893 as only around 40 shacks sitting up on stilts that were infested with swarms of fleas and mosquitoes. He even claimed to have even seen a cloud of mosquitoes extinguish an oil lamp! [64]

Hurricanes were another difficulty early settlers had to face in Florida. The Everglades and Chokoloskee communities was just beginning to recover from a hurricane that had struck in 1909 when they were decimated again in 1910. Only the highest points of the old Calusa shell mound stayed above flood levels. Farm fields were destroyed by the salt water storm surges, and most of the fresh water sources in the region were polluted, which devastated the area that already had so few fresh water springs or wells. Many inhabitants of the islands were forced to evacuate, leaving their homes to

---

64. National Park Service, 2015

the mercy of the storms. Tensions were high, and chaos reigned over the confusion of displacement. One notable event took place a few days after the storm: in the chaos of tragedy, vigilantes killed a man suspected of several murders. The killers were never punished. "Killing Mister Watson" by Peter Matthiesson portrays a fictionalized account of the event.

By the 1920s, towns like Fort Lauderdale, Miami, and Fort Myers were swarmed with tourists. Developers built roads, cut canals, and removed native mangroves to be replaced with palm trees. By building habitats for our own species, the developers destroyed those of many others.

This infuriated many people concerned about pollution and the environment. With help from early conservationists, scientists, and others passionate about the environment, the Everglades was named a national park in 1947 and given protection under the national government as a result.

Florida Panthers

Next to the Everglades are the freshwaters of Big Cypress Swamp. The water is necessary to the health of the Everglades, supporting the marine estuaries along Florida's southwest coast. The swamp is over 729,000 acres wide and is home to a diverse array of plants and wildlife, including the rare Florida panther, the state animal of Florida.

Seldom seen by human eyes, the panther stalks the prairies and pinelands of the Big Cypress Swamp. It is one of the biggest predators in Florida, efficiently keeping the wild game populations at healthy numbers.

Unlike most cats, the panther adapted to life around the swamp. It mostly hunts the white-tailed deer of South Florida but will also look for animals like wild hogs, rodents, armadillos, and birds to make its meals. While the panther feeds on small animals like these, it prefers larger meals in order to stay at optimum health. For example, a panther would need to eat 10 raccoons to receive the same nourishment as it would get from a single deer.

A Florida panther, one of the most endangered creatures in North America.

To stay fully nourished, a panther must kill about one deer's worth of food per week. The panther will lie in wait for hours, patiently stalking, waiting for the right moment to spring from its hiding spot and make its kill.

The powerful beast uses its retractable, razor-sharp claws to grab its prey before sinking its teeth into its neck, breaking the back of the animal. Panthers are most active during the dim hours of dawn and dusk, during which the light enhances their natural camouflage among the sawgrass.

Florida panthers are one of the most endangered creatures in North America, despite being the state animal. To protect livestock in the 1800s, panthers were hunted and killed for a bounty of $5 per cat. This mass elimination, combined with major habitat loss from human development in the Everglades, brought the panthers nearly to the brink of extinction. At one point, experts estimated that only 30 panthers were still alive in the wild.

The Endangered Species Act of 1973 finally allowed activists to begin saving the panthers. The cats were among the first animals in the United States to be placed on the list. Though the panthers were given federal protection, their numbers did not grow immediately. To spur reproduction and genetic diversity, a few female cougars were introduced from Texas into the remaining population of Florida. Their introduction allowed the Florida panther population to revitalize.

 Venice, Florida, is known as the Shark Tooth Capital of the World.[65]

There are currently around 80-100 cats left in the wild, a third of which live in the Big Cypress National Preserve. The biggest problem for the panthers today is habitat loss and highway collisions. 17 panthers were hit and killed by cars in South Florida in 2007.

To help prevent car fatalities, fencing has been installed along I-75 and SR-29. The fences guide wildlife to underpasses that allow them to cross the highways without being hit by passing traffic.[66]

---

65. 50 States.com, n.d.
66. National Park Service, n.d.

Chapter 7

The 1900s in Florida

> Here in Florida, we have something special we never enjoyed
> at Disneyland . . . the blessing of size. There's enough land
> here to hold all the ideas and plans we can possibly imagine.
> — Walt Disney

By 1925, Florida's population had grown to more than a million people thanks to the real estate boom. The economy was prospering, and many people wanted to sell land to make money. These land speculators, as they became known, bought cheap land and sold it for a big profit. These speculators often didn't even live in Florida, but rather hired others who would act in their stead to show land to interested buyers.

Some of those who bought the land didn't actually have enough money; they hoped for a quick turnaround and depended on the prices to keep continually rising. Laws that banned state income and inheritance taxes were written to attract more people to Florida, and horse and dog racing was implemented to attract gamblers to the state.

However, this land boom would not last forever. The cost of rent soared, and many people could not afford to pay. The demand for building materials overloaded the trains and railway systems, even shutting some down. The land prices stopped going up, but many people still could not afford to buy them. Now there were suddenly thousands of acres of land, but no one could afford them.[67]

The Great Depression Hits Florida

There may have been an economic boom in Florida during the 1920s, but the prosperity of the new century quickly ended. Two hurricanes had severely damaged southern Florida, causing severe flooding and wind damage, and killing thousands of people.

Then, an outbreak of Mediterranean fruit flies infested the state, killing off most of the citrus that was so important to Florida's economy. When the stock market fell in 1929, kicking off the Great Depression and hurting millions of Americans, Florida's financial situation went from bad to worse.

Across the nation, stock value plummeted and investors lost all of their money. They couldn't pay their bills, and very few jobs were open to the public. Banks closed and millions lost their life's savings. Families could not afford a place to live or even food. With no business, stores closed left and right. More than 90,000 families were affected by the Great Depression in Florida. During this time, one-quarter of the population of Florida received financial aid from the federal government.

Tourism during the winter months helped keep economy afloat as many people still drove to Florida to escape the cold. However, those who were without a job or a reasonable amount of money in their bank account were banned from the state. Police even patrolled the Florida border to ensure unwanted "tourists" stayed out. Florida lawmakers knew that the local

67. Florida Center for Instructional Technology, 2002

economy was barely able to sustain its own residents, much less the added burden of poor visitors who might choose to make their stay permanent.

The New Deal

In 1933, Franklin D. Roosevelt became president of the United States. He implemented the "New Deal," which created jobs to get the country and individuals back on their feet and restart the economy. One of these programs was called the Civilian Conservation Corps, or CCC. Young men from all over the U.S. lived in work camps, and around 40,000 of those were Florida natives. The men received food, clothing, and a place to stay while they sent their pay back home to their families. The Floridian CCC planted 13 million trees, created state parks and wildlife preserves, and built fire lines, schools, and federal buildings. Businesses began to redevelop, and the citrus industry and paper mills began to bring money into the state once again.

Another New Deal program was the WPA, or Works Progress Administration, which gave jobs to researchers, writers, and editors who might have otherwise been out of work. One of the Floridian writers who benefitted from this program was Zora Neal Hurston.[68]

Zora Neal Hurston

Over her career of more than 30 years, Zora Neal Hurston published four novels, two collections of folklore, an autobiography, various short stories, and multiple essays, articles, and plays. Some of her more famous works include "Their Eyes were Watching God" (1937) and "Mules and Men" (1935).

Hurston lived in Eatonville, six miles north of Orlando. Created in 1887, it was one of the first self-governing all-black municipalities, or townships,

---

68. Florida Center for Instructional Technology, 2002

in the United States. She sometimes said Eatonville was her birthplace and claimed it felt like home. Later on, in 1897, her father was elected the mayor of Eatonville.

Zora Neal Hurston, author of "How It Feels to Be Colored Me."

Hurston later used Eatonville as a setting for her stories. It was a place where African-Americans could live safely without fear of persecution or racism. Hurston described growing up in Eatonville in her 1928 essay, "How It Feels to Be Colored Me".

Although she went relatively unrecognized by much of the literary world, when author Alice Walker published "In Search of Zora Neale Hurston" in 1975, interest in Hurston's work was revived. After her death in 2001,

Hurtson's previously unpublished collection of 1920s folktales, "Every Tongue Got to Confess," was published.

Today, a Zora Neal Hurston Festival is held each January in Eatonville, where attendees celebrate the life and work of Zora Neale Hurston, the historic significance of Eatonville, and the cultural contributions made to the United States and world culture by people of African descent.[69]

Civil Rights Movement

The 1920s brought massive change to the United States, and with it came the rebirth of the Ku Klux Klan and racial violence. Florida did not escape the violence of the race riots that plagued the South — indeed, it saw more than its fair share. Race riots in towns like Ocoee and Rosewood tortured and killed blacks and whites, alike. As a result, many black residents fled these towns, never to return.

Between 1900 and 1930, around 140 black men and women were lynched (or executed without a trial) — the highest percentage based on population anywhere in the United States. Those who were lynched were accused of crimes such as rape and murder, but also of innocuous acts like insulting or flirting with a white women, or refusing to sell land. In most cases, the reasons for lynching a person were completely fabricated.

By the 1940s, racial tensions reached a head. Blacks who had returned from World War II had experienced life in the northern U.S. and Europe where there were no Jim Crow laws or Black Codes. They had seen life as it could be if they were treated as equals, or, at the very least, did not have to fear for their lives. They did not want to return to the South, where they would be subjected to racial intolerance once more.

---

69. Zora Festival, n.d.

It was then that the Civil Rights Movement was born. The NAACP, or National Association for the Advancement of Colored People, started a campaign called the "Double V". This name referred to the sought-after victory against racism oversees and at home. The campaign focused Florida's attention to the policy of southern segregation and racial prejudice.

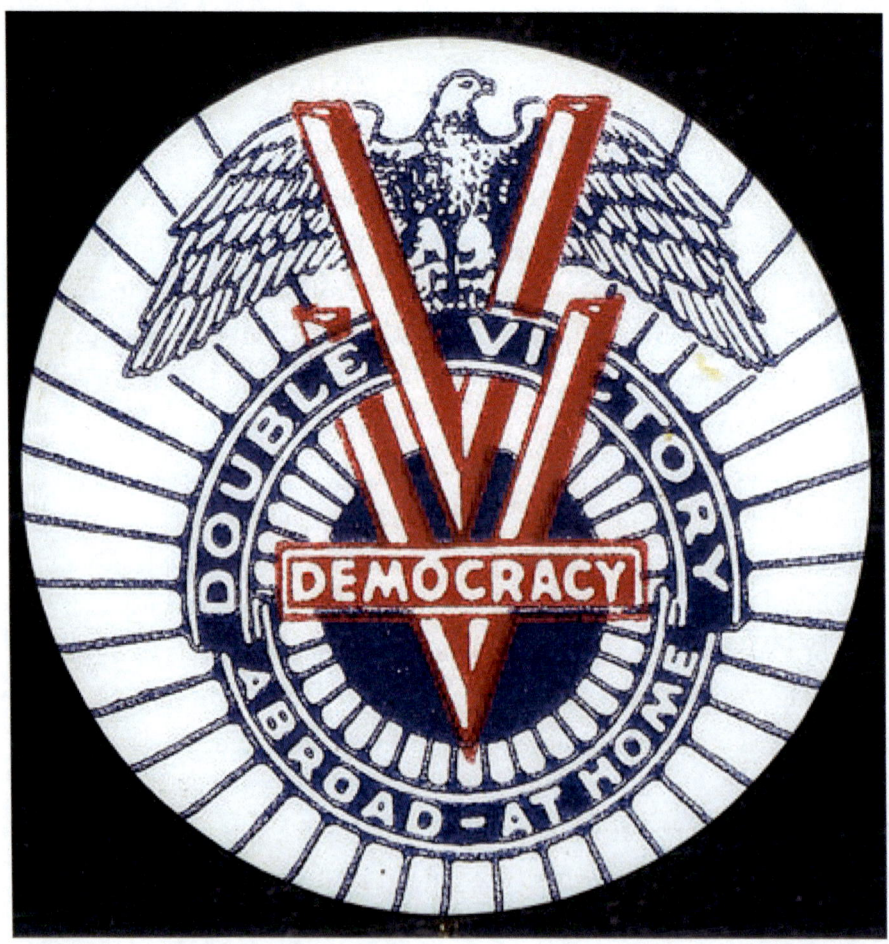

The NAACP logo for its "Double V" campaign.

Many whites were, at best, uncomfortable with social change and the prospect of equal rights for blacks, or, at worst, murderously angry at the very idea. The Ku Klux Klan terrorized black neighborhoods and brutally beat NAACP activists. Many members of the state government were also racist and some were even members of the Klan. They would often jail blacks who spoke out against unfair wages or hostile work conditions. Activist Harry T. Moore, along with his wife, were killed by members of the Klu Klux Klan on December 24, 1950 because of their involvement in developing an NAACP chapter in their community. An investigation uncovered a network of local government officials, police officers, and Klan members within the community, but no legal action was ever taken, and the murderers were never brought to justice.

In 1954, the U.S. Supreme Court decided to end racial segregation in schools. This decision swept across Florida and the South. But the end of segregation within schools was not enough; segregation pervaded almost every facet of public life, and civil rights activists wanted that to end. Two black women were arrested in Tallahassee in 1956 for sitting in the front section of a bus instead of in the back where 'colored people' had to sit. The entire African American community boycotted the bus system, refusing to ride, which lead to a revision of many unfair laws. Many Black Codes, previously so ingrained in the system, began to disappear.[70]

However, laws could not end racism completely. Dr. Martin Luther King, Jr. visited Florida in 1964 during his Southern Christian Leadership conference. He said it was the only time he had been afraid for his life. Marches in St. Augustine devolved into brutal violence between anti-segregation marchers and segregationist bystanders. A sit-in at a lunch counter, or protest where activists refuse to leave an area, resulted in the arrest of 16 people, including four children who were sent to reform school. Protests across the country later freed the children, although the Florida legislature

---

70. Florida Center for Instructional Technology, 2002

blamed black Muslims and northern agitators for inciting the incident in the first place.[71]

Eventually, the United States passed a law called the Civil Rights Act of 1964, which prohibited any form of segregation. The senators from Florida were against the bill and vowed to fight against it, but were defeated. In 1968, Joe Land Kershaw was elected as the first black man in the Florida House since the Reconstruction era.

Disney World Opens

Tourism has always been a vital part of Florida's economy, but one famous theme park cemented the state forever as a family vacation destination: Walt Disney World.

Walt Disney, who was responsible for many classic movies such as "Cinderella," "Peter Pan," "The Jungle Book," and many others, imagined Walt Disney World Resort in the early 1960s. He saw it as an opportunity for those living on and around the East Coast to enjoy the unique entertainment concepts which had become world-renowned at California's Disneyland.

In 1963, the planning team at WED Enterprises (now called Walt Disney Imagineering) designated Florida as the new home state of Walt Disney World. The warm, welcoming weather was the perfect climate to permit year-round visitors and, as the state was already ranked first in tourism, the decision was made for them. The location search was narrowed even further to Orlando the affordable, spacious land offered vast opportunity for exponential future growth.

---

71. Clark, 2014

California's Disneyland had only 450 acres, and Walt Disney wanted a larger area for Disneyworld so visitors could enjoy the resort in peace. Land acquisition began in 1964 and cost around $5.5 million. Today, Disneyworld is around 30,000 acres.

Disney World was announced to the world on November 16, 1965 at a press conference in Orlando. Walt described his dreams: his new park would be a unique, iconic vacation center that would welcome visitors from all over the world.

Walt put his plans into action, developing ideas and laying out philosophies for the new site. The company built Seven Seas Lagoon, a 200-acre lake, two 18-hole golf courses, and six lands of the Magic Kingdom, plus land and water transportation to connect the parks. The whole project cost around $400 million.

Before the park opened in 1971, 1 million guests visited in under 20 months to view drawings, concepts, and motion pictures of the impressive and anxiously-awaited vacation spot.

The grand opening of Disney World was October 23-25, 1971, with a gala concert by the 60-nation World Symphony Orchestra, a spectacular luau at Polynesian Village Resort, celebrity appearances and dedications, and an opening parade with a 1,000-member marching band directed by Meredith Wilson, who wrote the musical "Music Man".

A photo of the opening day of Disney World.

The population of the Disney theme parks in Florida on a single day is greater than the population of the entire state during the Civil War.[72]

The Space Race

As technology improved, the U.S. government began to try and conquer space. They began the search for a potential launch site for aircrafts and missiles. They would eventually find it in Florida.

President Harry Truman designated the Bana River Naval Air Station, near Titusville, as a testing facility in 1949, naming it Patrick Air Force Base. The next year, the first missile was launched from that location.

The U.S. military coordinated operations at the base for nearly 10 years, until the National Aeronautics and Space Administration (NASA) took over. Thousands of acres were added to the area that is now known as the Kennedy Space Center.

On July 29, 1969, astronauts who had launched from the Kennedy Space Center. landed on the moon. Neil Armstrong said, "That's one small step for man, one giant leap for mankind," during his first steps on the moon on live television, making history as millions of people watched on Earth.

The space program brought thousands of jobs to Florida, including scientists, engineers, technicians, and computer experts. However, not all shuttle launches went according to plan. Another live, history-making television event occurred during the Challenger explosion, when the space shuttle

---

72. Clark, 2014

broke apart only 73 seconds after launching from Cape Kennedy. Many looked on as the tragedy occurred in real-time.

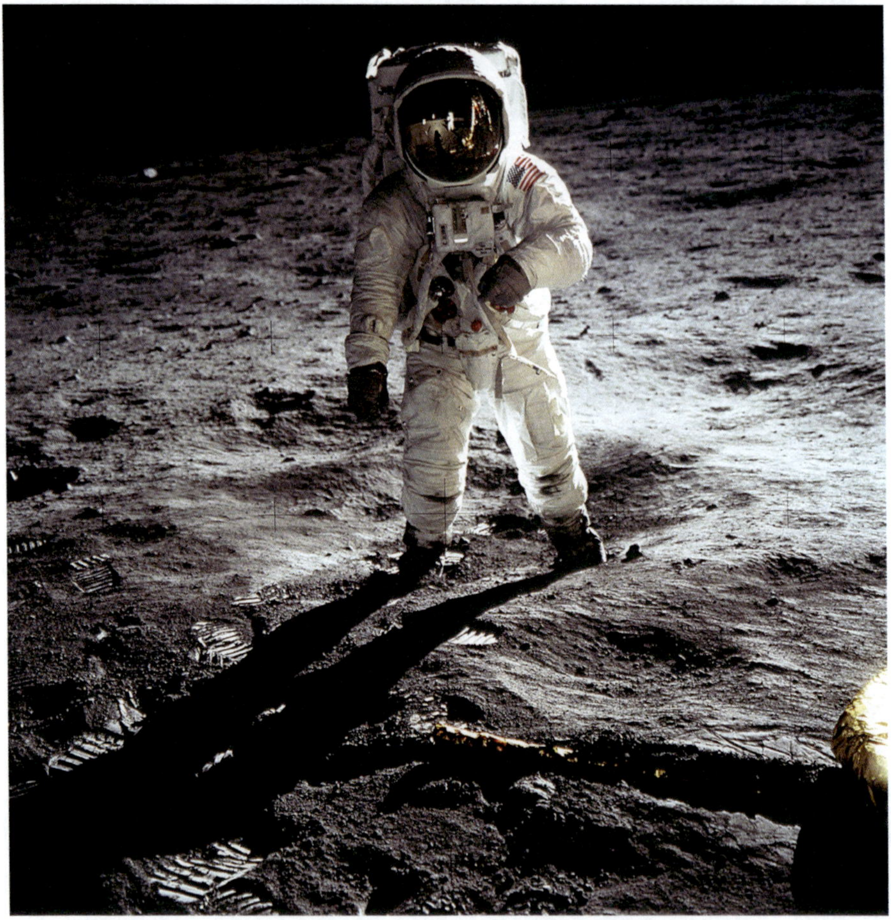

Neil Armstrong on the moon in 1969.

Plant City, FL, the Winter Strawberry Capital of the World, is home to the world's largest strawberry shortcake. The 827 square-foot, 6,000 pound cake was made in McCall Park on Feb. 19, 1999 and has been documented by Guinness World Records.[73]

73. "Florida Facts and Trivia", 2018

Chapter 8
Florida Today

> "August in Florida is God's way of reminding us who's in charge."
> — Blaize Clement

Florida grew and grew. It was the least populated state in the southern U.S. during World War II, but by the turn of the millennium, it was the fourth most populated state in the nation. In 2014, it officially became the third-largest state.

Retirees flock in massive numbers to the state, which has helped boost the population rates. In 1940, when Social Security was first implemented, retirees no longer had to depend on charity or family members for financial help. They could live on their own, receiving a stipend from the government. The checks alone were enough to send many recipients to Florida. Books like "How to Retire in Florida" (1947) became bestsellers and instructed readers on how to find a place to live in Florida or how to invest in some of its bountiful land.

Developers began building massive retirement communities. So many retirees moved to the warm, friendly Florida that the average age of the population actually increased. By 2014, Florida had one of the oldest populations in the country.

What's Next in Florida History?

Florida's long and storied history can be traced back earlier than the 1400s, but there is a lot to cover in recent history too.

The nation's attention was turned to Florida during the U.S. presidential election on November 7, 2000. It was an extremely close race and votes had to be recounted, leading to accusations of fraud and manipulation. The Florida secretary of state and supreme court, in a very controversial move, ended all recounts, and declared George W. Bush's victory over Al Gore by 537 votes. The entire process was incredibly controversial and resulted in calls for voting reform in Florida.[74]

Then, in 2012, an unarmed black teenager, Trayvon Martin, was shot and killed. This sparked protests across the country and led to conversations about gun control, the treatment of black men and women, and the "stand your ground law" that protects those who kill in self-defense.[75] Trayvon Martin's death is considered by many to be the start of the Black Lives Matter movement.

Florida has also captured news-worthy attention for more light-hearted matters as well. The Wizarding World of Harry Potter opened in Orlando in 2007, delighting visitors from all over the world with magic-themed rides, Butterbeer, and the ability to make their own wands.

74. George W. Bush, et al., Petitioners v. Albert Gore, Jr., et al., 2000.
75. CNN, 2018

Florida's incredibly diverse wildlife also continues to astound. A 12-foot alligator was spotted at a nature reserve in Lakeland, Florida. Nicknamed Humpback, it was one of the largest animals spotted in the area.[76]

These are only a few of the many news stories that have brought attention to the state in recent years. One of the biggest themes in Florida's news in the 21st century is the state of the environment. With growing concern for the preservation of the Everglades, ongoing climate change, and stronger than ever hurricanes, it's no wonder that a main priority for Florida's government is its natural surroundings.

Environment in Florida

While climate change is a topic of discussion everywhere in the U.S., it is one of significant importance to Florida. According to the Environmental Protection Agency (EPA), the peninsula's temperature has warmed more than one-degree Fahrenheit over the last 100 years. This may not sound like much, but this one degree has contributed to some huge physical changes in the natural landscape. The sea-level is rising about one inch every 10 years.

Within the next few decades, rising temperatures from climate change are likely to cause irreversible damage to coral reefs and increase the number of unpleasantly hot days per year.[77]

Heavy rainstorms and tropical storms have also become more intense during the past 20 years as a result of climate change. In 1992, Hurricane Andrew left 40 people dead and damaged or destroyed 100,000 homes with damages of around $20-30 billion. Much of South Florida's vegeta-

76. Tan, 2017
77. EPA, 2016

tion was damaged, and the storm nearly decimated the property insurance industry in the state because of the massive number of claims filed.

The hurricane season of 2004 battered the state with four major storms that resulted in as much as $40 billion in damage. Then in 2017, Hurricane Irma destroyed much of the Keys and lower portion of the mainland. A category 5 hurricane, Irma was one of the costliest hurricanes on record and caused at least 140 deaths.

Invasive Species

Florida has more invasive species than anywhere else in the world.[78] Invasive species are any non-native species to an area (either plant or animal), and can disrupt the ecosystem by eating native species and outcompeting them for food and other resources. They often disrupt the physical traits of an environment.

Some of the invasive species that plague Florida include wild boar, red fire ants, Cuban tree frogs, and kudzu. Overall, the pet industry was responsible for 84 percent of the 137 non-native species introduced from 1863-2010. In fact, 25 percent were traced to a single importer.[79]

The most notorious invader is the Burmese Python, first sighted in Everglades National Park in the 1980s. They were not officially recognized as a population until 2000, but the sightings in the area have increased with more than 300 sightings from 2008 to 2010.

These pythons are among the largest snakes on Earth. They can reach 23 feet or longer and can weigh up to 200 pounds. They live in trees when young, but transition to living predominantly on the ground in adulthood.

---

78. Prothero and Henry, 2013
79. Florida Today, 2011

They swim very well and can stay underwater for up to 30 minutes before returning to the surface for air.[80]

Burmese pythons eat birds, mammals, and reptiles in the Everglades, their arrival in Florida has had a major effect on numerous populations of native animals. Researchers estimate that at least 30,000 to 300,000 of these pythons currently occupy southern Florida. The importation of Burmese pythons was totally banned in the United States by the U.S. Department of the Interior in 2012 in an attempt to stem the growing population of the invasive species.[81] Hunts are also held in the Everglades each year to capture the pythons and help decrease their numbers, although the ecosystem there camouflages the snakes well and makes it hard for humans to find them.

80. National Geographic, n.d.
81. U.S. Fish and Wildlife Service, 2012

Conclusion

Florida's transition from vast, uncharted wilderness to one of the most popular states in the nation has been remarkable. From slaves and cotton groves to tourism and retirees, the changes that have consumed the state in the past 200 years are astounding.

It will be exciting to see what will come next in Florida's future. Remember, it has been a state for less than 200 years and has since made waves (sometimes literally) throughout the United States and its culture. Whether it's new theme parks, giant crocodiles, or the universally loved citrus production, Florida has cemented itself as one of the more unique states in the Union.

Ponce de Leon landed in Florida in 1513. Only 450 years or so later, man left Florida and landed on the moon. Florida's journey has been fascinating from the beginning — and it only continues to be more interesting.

I wonder what will come next!

Author's Note

There's a lot of Florida information I did not include in this book. I wanted to talk more about Rosewood, the Civil Rights Movement, the tourism that has so greatly impacted the state. I wanted to write more about influential women, about Cuban immigrants, about the national parks. There was so much I wanted to cover, and so much I could not finish. This book would be 1,000 pages long or more if I included everything from Florida's turbulent and exciting history!

Thankfully, there are so many more books about Florida out there about all of these aspects and more. A quick Google search will give you lots of information. I recommend finding the books I used in my bibliography and reading them for more facts and stories about Florida. I had a great time learning about the state, and hope to continue learning more about it throughout my life.

I am not from Florida, but I find its history fascinating. I hope you do too and will use my book as a launching point to learn more about this unique state. It has a past unlike any other, and the stories that can be told about Florida can be bizarre, funny, and devastatingly sad — or all three at the same time.

Timeline

1513: Ponce de Leon claimed to have discovered Florida

1564: Fort Caroline, north of Jacksonville, is established by the French

1565: Pedro Menéndez de Avilés establishes the city of St. Augustine

1565 September 20: Spanish attack Fort Caroline and kill most of the French, some escape

1763: Spain cedes Florida to England at end of the French and Indian War

1768: The colony of New Smyrna is established by Dr. Andrew Turnbull

1783 October 3: Treaty of Paris ends American Revolutionary War; England cedes Florida to Spain

1812: Republic of East Florida is established

1817–1818: First Seminole War

1821: Spain cedes Florida to United States

1835–1842: Second Seminole War

1845: Florida is admitted to the Union as the 27th U.S. state

1855–1858: Third Seminole War 1861: The Civil War begins

1865: Abraham Lincoln is assassinated and the Civil War ends

1877: Reconstruction ends

1914: The US enters World War I

1923: The town of Rosewood is destroyed after racially-motivated riots

1929: The Stock Market crashes, causing the Great Depression

1945: World War II begins

1964: The Civil Rights Act is passed and Segregation ends

1965: Disney World opens

1969: Three men are sent to the moon from Florida

2000: An election controversy in Florida elects George Bush to the presidency

2007: Harry Potter World opens, delighting fans worldwide

2012: Trayvon Martin is shot and killed

Glossary

Adelantado: Spanish for captain general

Caste system: a class structure that is determined by birth

Charter: a written grant by a country's legislative or sovereign power, by which an institution such as a company, college, or city is created and its rights and privileges defined

Chiefdom: kingdom

Crowd diseases: a disease where people who have contracted a disease and survived will from then on be immune to it

Conquistadors: a conqueror, especially one of the Spanish conquerors of Mexico and Peru in the 16th century

Detachment: a military unit

Estuary: a partially enclosed body of water with one or more rivers or streams flowing into it, with a free connection to the open sea

Inlet: a small arm of the sea, a lake, or a river

Homogenous: of the same kind; alike

Invasive species: non-native species to the area

Land speculators: those who bought land at cheap prices and sold them for a large profit

Maize: a Spanish term for corn

Missionary: a person sent on a religious mission, especially one sent to promote Christianity in a foreign country

Peat: an accumulation of partially decayed vegetation or organic matter

Secede: to withdraw formally from membership in a federal union, an alliance, or a political or religious organization

Sharecropping: a practice in which freed slaves pay the plantation owner rent on a portion of property by giving the owner a share of the crops grown on that land

Bibliography

Brands,H.W. *Andrew Jackson — His Life and Times.* Anchor Publishing, 2005. 489–93.

Brotemarkle, Ben. "Florida in the American Revolution" Florida Historical Society.2016

Canter Brown Jr., Florida's Black Public Officials, 1867-1924, (Tuscaloosa and London: The University of Alabama Press). 1998.

Clark, James. *A Concise History of Florida.* 2014. Arcadia Press. 9, 32-36

Clarke, Ransom. *The Surprising Narrative of Ransom Clarke.* Binghampton, N.Y. : J.R. Orton. 1839.

CNN. Trayvon Martin Shooting Fast Facts. 2018. https://www.cnn.com/2013/06/05/us/trayvon-martin-shooting-fast-facts/index.html

Covington, James W. 1993. *The Seminoles of Florida.* Gainesville, Florida: University Press of Florida. Pg 135-145

Cusick, James. The Other War of 1812: The Patriot War and the American Invasion of Spanish East Florida. University of Georgia Press. 2007. p. 49, 103, 261

Davis, Willian. "The History of the Short-Lived Independent Republic of Florida." Smithsonian. 2013. https://www.smithsonianmag.com/

history/the-history-of-the-short-lived-independent-republic-of
-florida-28056078/

Dunn, Marvin. *A History of Florida Through Black Eyes*. 2016. Createspace
Independent Publishing Platform. 49-58.

Environmental Protection Agency, "What Climate Change Means for Florida." 2016. https://19january2017snapshot.epa.gov/sites/production/
files/2016-09/documents/climate-change-fl.pdf

Explore Southern History. "The Republic of West Florida (1810)" 2013.
http://www.exploresouthernhistory.com/westflorida.html

Explore Southern History. "Prospect Bluff Historic Sites — Apalachicola
National Forest — Franklin County, Florida." 2017. http://www.
exploresouthernhistory.com/fortgadsden.html

Florida Center for Instructional Technology, "The Calusa: The Shell Indians." 2002. https://fcit.usf.edu/florida/lessons/calusa/calusa1.htm

Florida Center for Instructional Technology, "The Civil Rights Movement in
Florida." 2002. https://fcit.usf.edu/florida/lessons/cvl_rts/cvl_rts1.htm

Florida Center for Instructional Technology, "Florida's Land Boom." 2002.
https://fcit.usf.edu/florida/lessons/ld_boom/ld_boom1.htm

Florida Center for Instructional Technology. "The Great Depression
and the New Deal." 2002. https://fcit.usf.edu/florida/lessons/depress/
depress1.htm

Florida Center for Instructional Technology. "The Seminole Wars." 2002.
https://fcit.usf.edu/florida/lessons/sem_war/sem_war1.htm

Florida Center for Instructional Technology. "Reconstruction." 2002.
https://fcit.usf.edu/florida/lessons/reconst/reconst1.htm

Florida Center for Instructional Technology. "Tourism in Florida." 2002. https://fcit.usf.edu/florida/lessons/tourism/tourism1.pdf.

Florida Memory Blog. "Dr. Andrew Turnbull and the Origins of New Smyrna Beach." State Archives of Florida. 2014. http://www.floridamemory.com/blog/2014/05/14/dr-andrew-turnbull-and-the-origins-of-new-smyrna-beach/

Florida Today. "Invasive species traced to pet trade". Melbourne, Florida. September 16, 2011. pp. 4B.

Gannon, Michael. *The History of Florida.* University Press. 1996. Pgs 1-10, 55-75, 150, 153-159, 165, 172, 195-198, 201-202, 203-205, 206-207, 210-211,214-217, 232, 235-247.

George W. Bush, et al., Petitioners v. Albert Gore, Jr., et al., 531 U.S. 98 (2000).

Hann, John H. Indians of Central and South Florida: 1513–1763. University Press of Florida. (2003).

Howard, Bryan Clark. "The Flattest U.S. States? Not What You Think." National Geographic. 2014. https://news.nationalgeographic.com/news/2014/03/140314-flattest-states-geography-topography-science/

Manataka. "Timucua Indians of the Southeast." American Indian Council. https://www.manataka.org/page1232.html

Mahon, John K. *History of the Second Seminole War 1835-1842.* University of Florida Press. 1992. P. 106, 298

Martínez, Bartolomé. 1577.

Menéndez de Avilés, Pedro. 1565.

Menéndez de Avilés, Pedro. 1566. St. Augustine.

Missall, John and Mary. *The Seminole Wars: America's Longest Indian Conflict*. University Press of Florida. 2004. 76-91, 128-129, 152, 162-164.

National Geographic. "Burmese Python." N.d. https://www.national geographic.com/animals/reptiles/b/burmese-python/

National Park Service. "Developing the Everglades." 2015. https://www.nps.gov/ever/learn/historyculture/development.htm

50 States. "Florida Facts and Trivia. N.d. https://www.50states.com/facts/florida.htm

National Park Service. "Big Cyprus." N.d. https://www.nps.gov/bicy/planyourvisit/upload/Florida-Panther_FINAL_LORES-2.pdf

PBC History. "Florida Real Estate, Colonial Style." N.d. http://www.pbchistoryonline.org/middle-school-lessons/013-Britain%20in%20Florida/013-Transfer-Brits.htm

Prothero, Ariana and Henry, Kaylois. "Why Florida has the Most Invasive Species." 2013. http://wlrn.org/post/why-florida-has-most-invasive-species

Seminole Tribe. "History" n.d. https://www.semtribe.com/History/Introduction.aspx

Saxton, Rufus. letter to E.M. Stanton. 1863.

State of Florida, "Florida Quick Facts." N.d. http://www.stateofflorida.com/facts.aspx

Striepe, Becky. "Who Invented Sports Drinks?" March 5, 2013. https://science.howstuffworks.com/innovation/everyday-innovations/who-invented-sports-drinks1.htm

Tan, Avianne. "Giant Alligator Draws Crowds of Visitors to Florida Nature Reserve, Raises Concerns About Safety" ABCNews. 2017.

US Wars, "The Second Seminole War (1835-1842)". 2012. https://www. uswars.net/second-seminole-war/

Walt Disney World Magic. "Walt Disney World History. N.d. https:// www.wdwmagic.com/walt-disney-world-history.htm

Wynne, Lewis N. & Taylor, Robert A. (2001). Florida In The Civil War. Arcadia Publishing.

Zora! Festival Info. 2018. Zorafestival.org

Index